Treasury Department
January 18. 1792

There are various arrangements
between the Government and
the States, which will better
[ ] personal conference than
[ ]

request therefore that such

[ap]pear proper to the direction

The Founding Fathers

Engraving by John F. E. Prud'homme after a miniature, circa 1790, by Archibald Robertson

Hamilton

The Founding Fathers

ALEXANDER HAMILTON

A Biography in His Own Words

VOLUME 1

Edited by
MARY–JO KLINE

With an Introduction by
HAROLD C. SYRETT
Editor, *The Papers of Alexander Hamilton*

JOAN PATERSON KERR
Picture Editor

NEWSWEEK
New York

We dedicate this series of books to the memory of
Frederick S. Beebe
friend, mentor, and "Founding Father" of Newsweek Books

Alexander Hamilton, A Biography in His Own Words,
has been produced by the Newsweek Book Division:

Joseph L. Gardner, Editor

Janet Czarnetzki, Art Director

Thomas Froncek, Assistant Editor

Susan Storer, Picture Researcher

S. Arthur Dembner, Publisher

This book is based on Volumes 1–19 of *The Papers of Alexander Hamilton,*
edited by Harold C. Syrett and published by Columbia University Press.
The texts of documents to be published in forthcoming volumes of this edition
have been supplied by Mr. Syrett, and permission to reproduce excerpts
from these documents has been obtained from their owners.

ISBN: Clothbound Edition 0-88225-043-4; ISBN: Deluxe Edition 0-88225-044-2
Library of Congress Catalog Card Number 72-92140
Copyright © 1973 by Newsweek, Inc.
All rights reserved. Printed and bound in the United States of America
Endpapers: Hamilton to the President and Directors of the Bank of the United States,
January 18, 1792; HISTORICAL SOCIETY OF PENNSYLVANIA

Contents

Introduction

by Harold C. Syrett
Editor, The Papers of Alexander Hamilton

Despite differences in party, background, and ideology, many recent American political leaders have shared an almost pathological interest in how posterity will judge their accomplishments. Some of them have meticulously tried to preserve all that they have written and all that has been written to them, and on more than one occasion they have rushed into print in an apparent effort to set the record straight before historians have had an opportunity to examine that record. Every President of the United States since Franklin D. Roosevelt has arranged for the establishment of a special library to house his papers as well as those of many of his associates. Some Presidents have written their own versions of the events in which they were the principal participants, while more than one Chief Executive has appointed to his staff an academician whose responsibilities have presumably included that of court historian. Lesser figures in each administration, along with state and city officials, have published books and articles drawing on information that they had acquired in office. For those too inept or too lazy to write their memoirs, there has been no shortage of ghost writers and tape recorders. Most such efforts constitute in varying degrees a contribution to history, but all of them also represent a species of special pleading.

The Founding Fathers were also interested, if not obsessed, with the verdict of history. Although they seldom published their memoirs, many of them were careful to preserve their own records of the momentous times in which they lived. In this respect the first three Presidents of the United States are representative. George Washington had clerks or secretaries make letter book or letterpress copies of his letters, saved the letters that he received, and kept a diary that unfortunately contains little more than the names of visitors to Mount Vernon and reports on crops and the weather. John Adams was merely the first in his family to keep a diary and letter book and to preserve a vast amount of the avalanche of letters that descended on him during a long and eventful life. Like Washington and Adams, Thomas Jefferson retained the letters of his correspondents, but he also itemized in a ledger all his outgoing and incoming mail, and for part of his life he entered in the *Anas* his versions of each day's events and gossip. All three men left a legacy to mankind that in each case included a large corpus of papers telling what they and their contemporaries had done and thought during the formative years of the Republic.

As an immigrant, a parvenu, and an outspoken champion of aristocratic values,

Alexander Hamilton has always seemed the least typical of the Founding Fathers. In addition, he was often openly contemptuous of the opinions of his contemporaries, and there is little or no evidence that he was interested in telling future generations how they should view his record as a soldier, public servant, and political leader. He made no systematic effort to save the letters he received, and he did not copy in a letter book those that he sent. Nor did he record for his own amusement or for the edification of posterity accounts of his participation in the American Revolution, Continental Congress, New York legislature, Annapolis Convention, Constitutional Convention, New York ratifying convention, and Washington Administration.

It is difficult to avoid the conclusion that Hamilton was so concerned with the present that he gave little thought to what Americans would think of him in the future. Instead of diaries, he kept journals and ledgers that he considered either essential to his program of self-education or necessary for the day-to-day practice of his profession as a lawyer. During the American Revolution he filled his company's paybook with quotations and snippets of miscellaneous information from standard sources, and while studying for admission to the bar he wrote for his own use "Practical Proceedings in the Supreme Court of the State of New York." While practicing as a lawyer he kept cash books, which contain little beyond his legal and household accounts, and a register of cases, which lists some of the suits in which he served as an attorney from 1795 until his death. It is, perhaps, significant that the so-called Reynolds Pamphlet, his most famous—if not his only—example of special pleading, was designed to convince his contemporaries rather than their descendants that his lapses of private morality offered convincing proof of his public rectitude.

When Hamilton died on July 12, 1804, he left his widow an estate encumbered with debts and a collection of public and private papers that, according to his friend Gouverneur Morris, were "in wretched Disorder." In the remaining fifty years of her life Elizabeth Hamilton devoted her formidable energies to the care and feeding of her seven children and to an unrelenting campaign to perpetuate and enhance her husband's reputation through the exploitation of his writings. In her efforts to win for Hamilton the popular acclaim that she thought he deserved, she not unexpectedly met repeated rebuffs and discouragement, for she initiated her campaign during the ascendancy of the Virginia Dynasty and carried it on into and beyond the age of Jackson. But she was not easily discouraged; and before she died in 1854, she had not only acquired numerous copies and originals of Hamilton manuscripts to add to the collection that she had inherited, but she had also helped to persuade the United States Government to purchase and publish her husband's papers.

To Elizabeth Hamilton it seemed obvious that the most effective way to make Americans aware of her husband's achievements would be a biography based on his extant papers. At various times she commissioned—cajoled might be more accurate—James M. Mason, Joseph Hopkinson, Timothy Pickering, Francis Baylies, and Francis Hawks to write a biography. She was, however, uniformly unfortunate in her selection of authors. Some of them abandoned the project because of her interference; others backed out when it proved impossible to find a publisher; Pickering died before he could begin, let alone complete, the project; and Hawks used the papers entrusted to him to publish not a biography, but the first and only volume of a projected multivolumed edition of Hamilton's works. Understandably upset and disgusted with the outside talent that she had recruited, she turned to her own family and selected John C. Hamilton as his father's biographer.

In 1834 he published Volume I of *The Life of Alexander Hamilton*. Six years later he published two volumes under the same title, but "these...were nearly all burned while in the process of binding." Both editions covered only the early life of their subject, and it was not until 1857–60 that John C. Hamilton brought out his seven-volume edition of the *History of the Republic of the United States of America, as Traced in the Writings of Alexander Hamilton and of his Contemporaries.* Despite its obvious bias and leisurely pace, the *History of the Republic* remained the most authoritative biography of Hamilton until a century later when it was supplanted by Broadus Mitchell's *Alexander Hamilton.*

Although Elizabeth Hamilton did not live to see a complete and major biography of her husband, she made easier the task of his future biographers by searching for and finding manuscripts that were not part of the collection she had inherited. In these endeavors she enlisted the assistance of her sons, and James A. Hamilton and John C. Hamilton proved particularly helpful. All three wrote to Hamilton's contemporaries for materials, took frequent trips to talk with the owners of Hamilton manuscripts, and did not hesitate to use flattery or threats to attain their objectives. On one occasion Mrs. Hamilton resorted to the courts in her efforts to secure manuscripts she thought were rightfully hers. On another, James A. Hamilton wrote to Chief Justice John Marshall, the biographer of Washington, asking for papers in the Washington manuscripts "of which Genl Hamilton was the author." Not surprisingly, Marshall replied that the manuscripts in question were part of Washington's estate and that he had no authority to lend or give them away.

As she grew older, Elizabeth Hamilton became increasingly convinced that the most efficacious way of insuring her husband's fame was to have the Federal Government purchase and publish his papers. In June, 1848, when she was ninety-one, she wrote: "I have been for a very long time engaged in an application to Congress which in the probable course of human events will be the last, as it is the most interesting, business of my protracted life." She did not have long to wait, for on August 12, 1848, Congress provided in a routine appropriations bill twenty thousand dollars for the purchase "of the papers and manuscripts of the late Alexander Hamilton" and six thousand dollars for their "printing and publishing." Mrs. Hamilton did not record whether she found it ironical—or even distasteful—that this section of the bill was directly preceded by a similar provision appropriating the same amounts for the purchase and publication of the papers and manuscripts of Thomas Jefferson.

In 1849 Elizabeth Hamilton delivered her husband's manuscripts to the State Department, which subsequently transferred them to the Library of Congress. In 1850–51 John C. Hamilton published his seven-volume edition of *The Works of Alexander Hamilton*. The title page of these volumes announced that they were "published from the original manuscripts deposited in the Department of State, by order of the Joint Library Committee of Congress." Henry Cabot Lodge's edition of *The Works of Alexander Hamilton* in 1885 supplemented rather than supplanted John C. Hamilton's volumes, for although Lodge's edition contains some material not found in the earlier work, it also omits several letters and documents printed in the 1850–51 edition. Because John C. Hamilton's edition of his father's works includes most, but not all, of the items in the collection that his mother sold to the Government, it provides a rough guide to the range and nature of the papers that she had inherited and accumulated. During the past century the Hamilton papers in the Library of Congress have been augmented by several notable gifts and purchases. Perhaps the most important addition to the original collection were the manuscripts provided by Allan McLane Hamilton, Alexander Hamilton's grandson and a pioneering student of mental illness. These manuscripts, which deal mainly with Hamilton's family life and law practice, provided most of the material for Allan McLane Hamilton's *The Intimate Life of Alexander Hamilton,* which was published in 1910.

The collection of papers that Elizabeth Hamilton turned over to the Government in 1849 has more than justified the time and effort she expended on her husband's memory, for it has remained to this day an indispensable source for every serious student of Alexander Hamilton and the era that he helped to shape. It contains, however, less than a third of Hamilton's extant papers. Many of his most significant letters are in the papers of his contemporaries—most notably in those of George Washington—in the Library of Congress. Much, but not all, of his official correspondence and reports as Secretary of the Treasury are located in the National Archives. There are, moreover, large numbers of letters to and from Hamilton in the manuscript collections of such repositories as the New York Public Library, New-York Historical Society, Columbia University, Connecticut Historical Society, Massachusetts Historical Society, Historical Society of Pennsylvania, and the Henry E. Huntington Library. Many Hamilton manuscripts can also be found in the public and private archives of Canada, Great Britain (including four letters in Windsor Castle), Denmark, the Netherlands, and France. Finally, a relatively large number of Hamilton manuscripts, like those of most other famous men, are owned by individuals who have either inherited them or have purchased them for essentially the same reasons that motivate stamp collectors.

It is impossible, of course, even to estimate how many Hamilton manuscripts have been destroyed either by acts of nature or by misguided defenders of his and their own reputations. Some of his official correspondence as Secretary of the Treasury is known to have been burned in fires in buildings occupied by his successors during the first two decades of the new government. Moreover, one can only wonder what happened to those Hamilton manuscripts that Gouverneur Morris in 1807 "promised to examine and select" so that they would "not...fall into the hands of those who might publish them." The evidence also seems clear that Elizabeth Hamilton systematically searched out and destroyed all the letters that she had written to her husband. If she did not, the result was much the same, for not a single letter of hers to Alexander Hamilton has survived, while the collections in the Library of Congress and in other repositories contain countless letters that she wrote to others.

Several Hamilton documents have survived only in printed versions. For example, none of the manuscripts of Hamilton's contributions to *The Federalist* is known to exist, and the same applies to the many other articles he wrote for newspapers. Because most such articles by Hamilton and his contemporaries were signed by pseudonyms, it is difficult, if not impossible, to determine the name of the author in any given instance. The contents of such articles provide an unreliable guide to their authorship, for many of Hamilton's fellow Federalists not only shared his views but also contributed pseudonymous essays to the press. Nor does style provide an adequate clue to the identity of these writers. Among eighteenth-century polemicists the method of presentation was almost as standardized as that used in classical tragedies. It is true that statisticians with the aid of a computer have recently been able to determine the authorship of some of the issues of *The Federalist,* but to date no one has had either the money or the fortitude to apply the same techniques to the thousands of articles that filled the newspapers in the first years of the new nation.

Although scholars interested in the formative years of the American Republic have long realized that the bulk of Hamilton manuscripts in the Library of Congress represented only a fraction of what he had written and what had been written to him, it is only recently that a systematic attempt has been made to assemble and publish a comprehensive, annotated edition of Hamilton's papers. The idea for such an undertaking originated with President Nicholas Murray Butler of Columbia University, who during the last two decades of his life repeatedly called for a definitive edition of the papers of his institution's most famous alumnus. But first the Depression—for modern editorial projects are expensive—and then World War II and its aftermath intervened. Following Butler's death in 1947, John A. Krout, who served successively as professor of history, graduate dean, and provost at Columbia, worked tirelessly to turn Butler's proposal into a reality, and he more than any other individual deserves the major credit for the establishment at Columbia in 1955 of an editorial project known as the Papers of Alexander Hamilton. Initial financing was provided by the Rockefeller Foundation, with subsequent grants being furnished by Time Inc. and the Ford Foundation. A few weeks after the grant from the Rockefeller Foundation, an editorial staff began the task of gathering and editing Hamilton's papers.

In the years since 1955 the staff of the Papers of Alexander Hamilton has collected photocopies of approximately 19,000 documents, some of which contain no more than a single sentence, while others run for hundreds of pages. Although this may appear to be a sizable body of historical materials for the study of one man's life, it is in reality quite small when compared to the 63,000 items that have been accumulated by Julian P. Boyd as Editor of *The Papers of Thomas Jefferson.* The disparity in the two collections explains why Hamilton's writings will be published in approximately twenty-five volumes, while considerably more than twice that number will be needed for Jefferson's writings. No one—certainly not the editorial staff—can estimate what the relative lengths of the two editions might have been had Aaron Burr proved to be the less efficient duelist.

Each document—or more accurately each copy of a document—arriving at the office of the Papers of Alexander Hamilton must be catalogued and typed, and then the typescript has to be checked and double checked for accuracy. Until quite recently accurate transcription more often than not represented the final step in the editorial process. For example, almost all the multivolumed editions of *Works* or *Letters* that were published in the nineteenth century contain nothing more than the texts of documents. Even John C. Fitzpatrick's thirty-nine-volume edition of the *Writings of George Washington,* published between 1931 and 1944, provides the reader with little or no annotation for what are some of the most important sources of eighteenth-century American history. Present-day editors of historical documents are, however, neither lazy nor reticent, and there are some instances in which the editor's footnotes take up more space than the materials that they are designed to explain or illuminate. In the volumes of *The Papers of Alexander Hamilton* that have been published to date an attempt has been made to find some middle ground between scarcity and abundance.

The Papers of Alexander Hamilton present only a partial view of their subject's life, for they treat only in the most cursory fashion his career as an attorney—a career in which he spent approximately the same number of years as he did as a soldier and officeholder and in which his contributions were in many respects as notable as those he made as a public official and political leader. With these facts in mind Columbia University in 1960 established the Legal Papers of Alexander Hamilton to collect, edit, and publish a "documentary reconstruction of Hamilton's professional life" in a "period when the law was in rapid process of change and when the outcome of any juristic controversy depended as well upon a lawyer's mastery of pleading as upon his powers of mastery." Under the editorship of Julius Goebel, Jr., and the sponsorship of the William Nelson Cromwell Foundation, this project has published two volumes of a projected three-volume edition of *The Law Practice of Alexander Hamilton*. Based in large part on manuscripts in Hamilton's papers in the Library of Congress and on the surviving judicial records of city, state, and Federal courts, *The Law Practice of Alexander Hamilton*—to quote from its scholarly critics—"blazes a new trail in the field of biographical research and exposition," "imparts a totally new set of dimensions to the image of Alexander Hamilton," and "takes its place...as an adornment to scholarship and a lasting memorial to the patience and good sense of its editor."

In preparing the present biography of Alexander Hamilton, Mary-Jo Kline has for the most part used the materials printed in *The Papers of Alexander Hamilton* and *The Law Practice of Alexander Hamilton* and the papers that will appear in the subsequent volumes in these two editions of Hamilton's writings. Whenever possible she has permitted Hamilton and his contemporaries to speak for themselves. The result is a felicitous and penetrating account of Hamilton and his times that will enable the reader to draw his own conclusions concerning one of the most significant and controversial figures in the entire history of the United States.

EDITORIAL NOTE

Most of the Hamilton writings reprinted in this biography have been excerpted from the longer original documents being published in their entirety by Columbia University Press. Omissions at the beginning or ending of a document are indicated by ellipses only if the extract begins or ends in the middle of a sentence; omissions within a quoted passage are also indicated by ellipses. The original spellings have been retained; editorial insertions are set within square brackets

Chronology of Hamilton and His Times

Alexander Hamilton born in Danish West Indies	1755?
	1765 British Stamp Act brings first major Colonial protests
Begins working for Nicholas Cruger in St. Croix	1768
Sails for North America, fall or winter, 1772–73	1772 Samuel Adams organizes new committees of correspondence
Enters King's College (now Columbia University), New York City; publishes first pamphlet, "A Full Vindication of the Measures of the Congress . . ."	1774 Parliament passes Coercive Acts; First Continental Congress meets
Publishes "The Farmer Refuted"	1775 Battles of Lexington and Concord
Named Captain of New York Provincial Artillery	1776 Declaration of Independence signed; British capture Long Island and New York City
Becomes Washington's aide and lieutenant colonel in Continental Army; present during American defeats at Brandywine Creek and Germantown; winters with Army at Valley Forge	1777 Howe takes Philadelphia; Burgoyne surrenders to the Americans at Saratoga; Articles of Confederation adopted
Sees action at Battle of Monmouth Court House	1778 American alliance with France
Serves with Washington in New Jersey; combats rumors that he had been fomenting an Army rebellion against Congress	1779 Spain declares war on England; Iroquois Confederacy subdued by American expedition; naval victory of John Paul Jones
Becomes involved in movement for governmental reforms; is denied request for field duty; marries Elizabeth Schuyler, December 14	1780 Charleston falls to British; French force under Rochambeau reaches Newport; Battle of Camden; Arnold's treason revealed
Breaks with Washington, resigns from Army; publishes *Continentalist* essays; rejoins Army and leads assault on British redoubt at Yorktown	1781 Articles of Confederation ratified; executive departments created; Cornwallis surrenders at Yorktown
Birth of first son, Philip; resigns from Army; serves as New York receiver of Continental taxes; admitted to bar; represents New York in Congress	1782 Carleton succeeds Howe as British commander; preliminary articles of peace signed at Paris
Leads congressional fight for impost and half pay; moves family to New York City; opens first law office	1783 Newburgh Addresses circulated; threat of Army mutiny forces Congress to flee Philadelphia; definitive peace treaty signed at Paris; Britain recognizes American independence
Publishes *Letters from Phocion;* helps organize Bank of New York; serves as counsel in *Rutgers* v. *Waddington,* case testing supremacy of United States law over laws of states	1784 Congress makes New York temporary capital; diplomatic corps reorganized; John Jay becomes Secretary for Foreign Affairs
Elected to New York Assembly; serves as New York delegate to Annapolis Convention	1786 Annapolis Convention; Shays' Rebellion
Attends Constitutional Convention at Philadelphia; begins publishing *The Federalist* essays	1787 Constitution ratified by first three states

Leads Federalists at New York's ratifying convention at Poughkeepsie; elected to Continental Congress	1788	Constitution adopted, having been ratified by eleven states; first Federal elections held
Named Secretary of the Treasury	1789	New Federal Government organized; Washington inaugurated as President, Adams as Vice President; beginning of French Revolution
Moves with wife and four children to Philadelphia; submits reports on public credit and a national bank; leads battle for Federal assumption of state debts	1790	Jefferson takes office as Secretary of State; Congress assumes state debts and agrees to locate the national capital in the South
Defends constitutionality of a national bank; begins affair with Maria Reynolds; submits report on manufactures	1791	Legislative Assembly governs France; Congress enacts whiskey excise; growth of Republican opposition in Congress
Defends policies in the press; accused privately of misdirecting public funds, denies charges, confessing to affair with Mrs. Reynolds and use of own funds to pay blackmail	1792	New York financial panic; war of the First Coalition of European powers against France; National Convention replaces Legislative Assembly in France, monarchy abolished
Opponents' attempts at censure defeated in Congress; informs President of intention to resign; works to undermine support for France during Citizen Genêt affair; stricken, with wife, during yellow fever epidemic	1793	Louis XVI executed; Reign of Terror; France declares war on Britain, Holland, and Spain; United States proclaims neutrality; Randolph becomes Secretary of State
Treasury Department investigated by House committee; Hamilton leads call for military expedition to suppress Whisky Rebellion; takes the field against the rebels	1794	Growing friction between the United States and Britain; Jay named special envoy to England; Jay's treaty concluded; led by Kosciusko, Poles revolt against Russia
Submits last report on public credit; resigns from Cabinet; leads fight for Jay's treaty; publishes first *Camillus* essay	1795	French Directory succeeds National Convention; Jay's treaty ratified; signing of Pinckney's treaty with Spain
Argues case for "carriage" tax; drafts Washington's Farewell Address	1796	Adams elected President, Jefferson elected Vice President
Works for support of peace commission; publishes pamphlet on the Reynolds affair	1797	Adams names peace commission to France; XYZ affair revealed
Named Major General and Inspector General of the Army	1798	Beginning of America's Quasi War with France; Alien and Sedition Acts adopted
Urges military expedition to suppress Fries' Rebellion; influence over Cabinet members brings clash with Adams; proposals for reorganization of Army accepted by Congress	1799	War of the Second Coalition against France; death of Washington; Directory replaced by Consulate of Napoleon Bonaparte
Disbands troops, resigns Army command; circulates letter opposing Adams; supports Jefferson after electoral tie with Burr	1800	Treaty of Mortefontaine ends Quasi War with France; Federalists Adams and Pinckney opposed by Jefferson and Burr in presidential election; capital moved to District of Columbia
Son Philip dies in duel; publishes *The Examination*	1801	House chooses Jefferson to be President, Burr to be Vice President; beginning of Tripolitan War
Proposes reform of Federalist party; moves family to the Grange in upper Manhattan	1802	
Defends freedom of the press in *People* v. *Crosswell*; begins campaign against Aaron Burr; wounded in duel with Burr, Alexander Hamilton dies, July 12; buried in Trinity churchyard in lower Manhattan	1804	Aaron Burr defeated for Governor of New York; Napoleon begins rule as Emperor of France, 1804–14

Pay Roll for the Colony Company of Artillery commanded by Alexander Hamilton from March 6 to April 1st 1776 — Viz.

Mens Names	Time when pay was drawn	Left the service when and finished	Time due the Company	Stop to the Month	Amount Wages	Money due the Company	Ballance due the Company	Left by Deserter	Deserted by Deserter
Amount brought over					161. 12. 7½				
March 15 John Hammond			17 days	5/6	1. 10. 1½				
Lawrence Farguson			17 d°	d°	1. 10. 1½				
16 James McGeer			16 d°	d°	1. 8. 4				
William Scott			16 d°	d°	1. 8. 4				
17 Uriah Crawford			15 d°	d°	1. 6. 6½				
21 Aaron Robins			11 d°	d°	19. 5½				
23 Joseph Mason			9 d°	d°	15. 11½				
27 Thomas Delancy			5 d°	d°	8. 10½				
Isaac Sayers			5 d°	d°	8. 10½				
28 Joseph Child			4 d°	d°	7. 1.				
30 Stephen Norris			2 d°	d°	3. 6½				
Joseph Brooks			2 d°	d°	3. 6½				
					172. 3. 5½				

E. E. New York April 1. 1776

A Hamilton Capt

New York April 1. 1776 Received of Colonel McDougall One hundred and seventy two pounds, three shillings and five pence half penny, for the pay of the Commissioned, Non commissioned officers and privates of my company to the first instant, for which I have given three other receipts —

£ 172. 3. 5½

Alex Hamilton Capt

Pay Roll For the Colony Company of Artillery From March 6. to April 1. 1776 —

N° 11

See List

McDougall Papers

Captain Alexander Hamilton's payroll record of March, 1776, for his New York artillery company in the Revolution

Chapter 1

Up from Obscurity

In the first twenty-one years of his life, Alexander Hamilton struggled for a chance to prove himself and gain recognition of his abilities. By chance, this struggle brought him to the North American Colonies at the moment when loyal British subjects had begun to explore the idea of creating a new nation. Of all the Founding Fathers, Hamilton was especially suited to fight for a new society where men could live together free of ancient customs and outworn prejudices. An illegitimate child, Hamilton had neither family, fortune, nor tradition to call his own. Indeed, historians are not even sure of the time or place of his birth.

To the best of our knowledge, the future American statesman was born on one of the British Virgin Islands, in the Leeward group of the West Indies, probably in January, 1755. Several years before, his mother, Rachel Fawcett Lavien, had left her husband to become the common-law wife of James Hamilton, a Scottish merchant. For a time, young Alexander and his older brother, James, had an apparently normal family life. But in 1765 their father decided to go his own way, leaving Rachel Lavien and her two illegitimate sons to fend for themselves. Rachel quickly proved, however, that she had a better head for business than her bankrupt "husband." For three years she operated a prosperous store on the Danish island of St. Croix, but her efforts to provide for her boys were short-lived. She died in February, 1768, and the courts awarded all her property to the son she had borne by her estranged husband, John Lavien. In effect, Alexander and his brother were orphaned at the ages of thirteen and fifteen. Still, although their charming but irresponsible father did nothing to help them, the boys found that their mother had given them a particularly valuable legacy—the example of her pride and hard work. In short order, young James found work as an apprentice to a carpenter, and Alexander became a clerk in the office of Nicholas Cruger, a New York merchant who operated a trading firm in St. Croix.

The circumstances of Hamilton's boyhood years make it difficult to present a balanced picture of his early life in his own words. For a man's youthful writings to survive there must be people willing to save such documents—proud parents to treasure his school exercise books, close friends to preserve his first letters. It is almost equally important that a future statesman remain in one place during his early years of obscurity, so that historians will know where to look for records of his boyhood and young manhood. Obviously, Hamilton's youth did not lend itself to the preservation of his manuscripts. Most of the letters that have survived from this period are business correspondence copied in his employer's letter books. A number of poems and articles published in various Colonial newspapers have also been preserved. But the only personal letter that has survived from the time when Hamilton lived in St. Croix is one that he sent to Edward Stevens, a young friend who had been sent to school in New York. Though in general we can only guess at the thoughts of this lonely, brilliant boy, his letter to "Ned" gave a vivid picture of the hopes and dreams that the fourteen-year-old Hamilton concealed as he worked over Nicholas Cruger's account books.

Young Hamilton's letter to his friend, Edward (Ned) Stevens

St Croix Novemr. 11th 1769

This just serves to acknowledge receipt of yours per Cap Lowndes which was delivered me Yesterday. . . . As to what you say respecting your having soon the happiness of seeing us all, I wish, for an accomplishment of your hopes provided they are Concomitant with your welfare, otherwise not, tho doubt whether I shall be Present or not for to confess my weakness, Ned, my Ambition is prevalent that I contemn the grov'ling and condition of a Clerk or the like, to which my Fortune &c. condemns me and would willingly risk my life tho' not my Character to exalt my Station. Im confident, Ned that my Youth excludes me from any hopes of immediate Preferment nor do I desire it, but I mean to prepare the way for futurity. Im no Philosopher you see and may be jusly said to Build Castles in the Air. My Folly makes me ashamd and beg youll Conceal it, yet Neddy we have seen such Schemes successfull when the Projector is Constant I shall Conclude saying I wish there was a War.

I am D[ea]r Edward Yours

ALEX HAMILTON

By early 1771, Hamilton had begun to experiment with a means to "prepare the way for futurity." On April 6, the printer of the *Royal Danish American Gazette*, St. Croix's English-language newspaper, published the following contribution from Nicholas Cruger's young clerk.

[April, 1771]

I am a youth about seventeen, and consequently such an attempt as this must be presumptuous; but if, upon perusal, you think the following piece worthy of a place in your paper, by inserting it you'll much oblige
Your obedient servant,

A.H.

Just Imported from Quebeck, in the Brigt. Harriot, and to be sold by the subscriber, at Mr. Barry's Tavern, very reasonable for cash or crop pay,

A CARGO OF EXCELLENT DRAUGHT AND SADDLE HORSES, single and in pairs.—Also, English Pease, Brown Bread, Pickled and Smoaked Salmon.
BENEDICT ARNOLD.
Christianstæd, December 11, 1773.

In 1773 a St. Croix newspaper ran this advertisement from a West Indies horse trader with a name later famous, Benedict Arnold.

In yonder mead my love I found
Beside a murm'ring brook reclin'd:
Her pretty lambkins dancing round
Secure in harmless bliss.
I bad the waters gently glide,
And vainly hush'd the heedless wind,
Then softly kneeling by her side,
I stole a silent kiss—

She wak'd, and rising sweetly blush'd
By far more artless than the dove:
With eager haste I onward rush'd,
And clasp'd her in my arms;
Encircled thus in fond embrace
Our panting hearts beat mutual love—
A rosy-red o'er spread her face
And brighten'd all her charms.

Silent she stood, and sigh'd consent
To every tender kiss I gave;
I closely urg'd—to church we went,
And hymen join'd our hands.
Ye swains behold my bliss complete;
No longer then your own delay;
Believe me love is doubly sweet
In wedlocks holy bands.—

As the year 1771 wore on, Hamilton had little time for poetry, but he found an opportunity to prove his abilities in another area. On October 15, Nicholas Cruger sailed to New York "by reason of a very ill state of health," and his sixteen-year-old clerk was left in charge of business in St. Croix. Since Cruger's father and brothers owned trading firms in New York, England, and various West Indian ports, the office in St. Croix was part of a family network of international scope. During Cruger's absence, young Alexander Hamilton was responsible for making the daily decisions that such a business entailed. For five months, he handled the firm's correspondence and carried out his employer's orders. This letter to Nicholas Cruger gave a hint of the problems that Hamilton faced.

Heads and tails of a piece of eight, a Spanish silver dollar

St Croix Novem. 12 1771

Markets are just the same excepting in the price of Butter which is now reducd.... Your Philadelphia flour is realy very bad, being of a most swarthy complexion & withal very untractable; the Bakers complain that they cannot by any means get it to rise. Wherefore & in consideration of the quantity of flour at Market and the little demand for it I have some thought not to refuse 8½ [pieces of eight] from any good person that will give it.... Upon opening several barrels I have observ'd a kind of Worm very common in flour about the surface, which is an indication of Age. It could not have been very new when twas shipd and for all these reasons I conceive it highly necessary to lessen the price or probably I may be oblig'd in the end to sell it at a much greater disadvantage. ...

No appearance of the Thunderbolt nor no News from Curracoa.

The *Thunderbolt* mentioned above was a sloop owned by Cruger and his partners and commanded by Captain William Newton. When the ship reached St. Croix in mid-November, Hamilton handled the details of her voyage to the Dutch island of Curaçao and gave the captain his orders in the following letter.

WEST INDIES,
agreeable to the
most approved
MAPS and CHARTS,
M^rKitchen.

A map decoration, circa 1770, advertises the West Indies trade.

St Croix Nov. 16 1771

Here with I give you all your dispatches & desire youll proceed immediately to Curracoa. You are to deliver your Cargo there to Teleman Cruger Esqr. agreeable to your Bill Lading, whose conditions you must follow in every respect concerning the disposal of your Vessell after your arrival. You know it is intended that you shall go from thence to the Main for a load of Mules & I must beg if you do, you'll be very choice in Quality of your Mules and bring as many as your Vessell can conveniently contain. By all means take in a large supply of provendor. Remember you are to make three trips this Season & unless you are very diligent, you will be too late as our Crops will be early in.

Take care to avoid the Gaurda Costos [Spanish customs officials]. I place an intire reliance upon the prudence of your Conduct.

For ten weeks, Hamilton anxiously awaited Newton's return from Curaçao with his cargo of mules from the Spanish Main. On January 29, 1772, the sloop reached St. Croix, and Hamilton faced more problems, as he reported to Tileman Cruger, his employer's brother in Curaçao.

St Croix Febru 1, 1772

Two days ago Capt Newton deliverd me your favour without date & 41 Mules in such order that I have been oblig'd to send all of them to pasture, and of which I expect at least a third will die. The highest offer made me for 20 of the best was 70 ps. [pieces of eight], whereas if they had been in good order I could readily have obtain'd £40 round, which I all along entertaind the most sanguine hopes of. Thus you see how unfortunate the Thunderbolts first Voyage has been. But we must try a second time. Accordingly I have put on Board her some Codfish, Rum & Bread as per Inclosd Bill Lading & wish them to a good Market.

Capt Newton is to supply himself with Grass on his way down & I must beg the favour of you by all means to buy or hire him a few Guns which is agreeable to Mr. Crugers directions to me. I should do it here if it were possible but there are none to be had upon any terms whatever & it would be undoubtedly a great pity that such a Vessell should be lost for the want of them....

It is thought by Judges that the Sloop Thunderbolt ought to carry 60 Mules. If you think so, please to desire the Capt to do it. I have mentioned it to him, but he insists that 48 are as many as she can conveniently hold. The more she brings the better. But I do not pretend to be a Judge of the matter & therefore leave it to you. But Without the utmost dispatch her second Voyage may miscarry like the first. Please to send by the Sloops return a full state of accounts between you & Mr. Cruger that I may enter all things properly.

A busy, palm-lined road on St. Croix

Despite the failure of Newton's first voyage, Hamilton immediately sent the captain back on another expedition. Three weeks after the *Thunderbolt* set sail for the second time, Hamilton dispatched this account of the sloop's misadventures to Nicholas Cruger in New York.

St Croix February 24 1772

Your Sloop Thunderbolt arrivd here the 29th of the preceding Month with 41 More Skeletons. A worse parcel of Mules never was seen; she took in at first 48 & lost 7

For COPENHAGEN,
The Ship Valley of Roses
Capt. Peter Andreas Janſen,

WILL be ready to sail the beginning of next month; therefore all Gentlemen who have any goods to ship on board said vessel, are desired to have them ready by the end of the present month.

∴ All persons who have had any dealings with the said PETER ANDREAS JANSEN, are entreated to pay off their accounts before the above mentioned time, else he will be under the disagreeable necessity of suing them at a special court.

St. Croix, August 14, 1770.

Above: A captain announces the departure of his merchant ship from St. Croix; opposite: Hamilton's letter describing the hurricane that struck the island in 1772

on the passage. I sent all that were able to walk to pasture, in Number 33. The other 8 could hardly stand for 2 Minutes together & in spite of the greatest care 4 of them are now in Limbo. The Surviving 4 I think are out of Danger, and shall likewise be shortly sent to pasture. I refusd two great offers made me upon their first landing to Wit 70 ps. a head for the Choice of 20, and 15 ps. a Head for the abovementioned Invalids, which may give you a proper idea of the condition they were in. Taking this along with it—that if they had been such as we had reason to hope they would be—I could with pleasure have had £40 round, so unfortunate has the Voyage been. However by sending them to pasture I expect to get £100 round for those now alive. 17 are already gone at that price and as they recruit fast the rest I hope will soon go at the same.... The Sloop was 27 days on her passage from the Main—not for want of swiftness, for tis now known she Sails well, but from continual Calms & the little wind she had was quite against her. Capt Newton seemd to be much concernd at his Ill luck tho I believe he had done all in his power to make the voyage Successful. But no Man can command the Winds. The Mules were pretty well chosen & had been once a good parcel. I receivd only a few lines from your Brother; no Sales nor anything else; he excusd himself being Sick. I desird him as directed to furnish the Sloop with a few Guns but she went intirely defenceless to the Main; notwithstanding several Vessells had been obligd to put back to get out of the way of the Launches with which the Coast swarms. When Capt Newton urgd him to hire a few Guns for the Sloop He replied to this effect—that I only had mentiond the matter to him but that you had never said a word about it. This last time I mentiond it again & begd the Captain to hire 4 Guns himself if your Brother did not which he has promisd to do. The Expence will not be above 15. or 20 ps., and one escape may not be followd by a second, neither do I see any reason to run the risque of it.

Although Hamilton had made a favorable impression on the Crugers and their business associates during the winter of 1771–72, he returned to "the grov'ling and condition of a Clerk" when Nicholas Cruger came back to St. Croix in March. But while he dutifully copied

Cruger's letters during the spring and summer, the boy still kept his eyes open for his own "futurity." It was a natural disaster, however, not a war (as he had predicted to Edward Stevens in 1769) that gave Hamilton his chance to escape ledgers and account books. On August 31, 1772, a hurricane swept St. Croix, and a few days later Hamilton wrote an account of the storm in a letter to his father. A copy of the letter reached Hugh Knox, a Presbyterian minister and journalist on the island, and Knox arranged to have the letter published in the *Royal Danish American Gazette* of October 3, 1772. It was this letter that won the boy local fame and an opportunity to leave Nicholas Cruger's countinghouse.

St. Croix, Sept. 6, 1772

I take up my pen just to give you an imperfect account of one of the most dreadful Hurricanes that memory or any records whatever can trace, which happened here on the 31st ultimo at night.

It began about dusk, at North, and raged very violently till ten o'clock. Then ensued a sudden and unexpected interval, which lasted about an hour. Meanwhile the wind was shifting round to the South West point, from whence it returned with redoubled fury and continued so 'till near three o'clock in the morning. Good God! what horror and destruction. Its impossible for me to describe or you to form any idea of it. It seemed as if a total dissolution of nature was taking place. The roaring of the sea and wind, fiery meteors flying about it in the air, the prodigious glare of almost perpetual lightning, the crash of the falling houses, and the ear-piercing shrieks of the distressed, were sufficient to strike astonishment into Angels. A great part of the buildings throughout the Island are levelled to the ground, almost all the rest very much shattered; several persons killed and numbers utterly ruined; whole families running about the streets, unknowing where to find a place of shelter; the sick exposed to the keeness of water and air without a bed to lie upon, or a dry covering to their bodies; and our harbours entirely bare. In a word, misery, in all its most hideous shapes, spread over the whole face of the country. A strong smell of gunpowder added somewhat to the terrors of the night; and it was observed that the rain was surprizingly salt. Indeed the water is so brackish and full of sulphur that there is hardly any drinking it. . . .

[After this factual account of the storm, Hamilton turned to his own "reflections and feelings on this frightful and melancholy occasion."]

Where now, oh! vile worm, is all thy boasted fortitude and resolution? What is become of thine arrogance and self sufficiency? Why dost thou tremble and stand aghast? How humble, how helpless, how contemptible you now appear....

Death comes rushing on in triumph veiled in a mantle of tenfold darkness. His unrelenting scythe, pointed, and ready for the stroke. On his right hand sits destruction, hurling the winds and belching forth flames: Calamity on his left threatening famine disease and distress of all kinds. And Oh! thou wretch, look still a little further; see the gulph of eternal misery open. There mayest thou shortly plunge—the just reward of thy vileness. Alas! whither canst thou fly? Where hide thyself? Thou canst not call upon thy God; thy life has been a continual warfare with him....

Thus did I reflect, and thus at every gust of the wind, did I conclude, 'till it pleased the Almighty to allay it. Nor did my emotions proceed either from the suggestions of too much natural fear, or a conscience over-burthened with crimes of an uncommon cast. I thank God, this was not the case. The scenes of horror exhibited around us, naturally awakened such ideas in every thinking breast, and aggravated the deformity of every failing of our lives.

[Although this letter was supposedly only a private message for his father, Alexander Hamilton closed his account of the hurricane with an appeal for public charity and high praise for the Governor General.]

But see, the Lord relents. He hears our prayer. The Lightning ceases. The winds are appeased. The warring elements are reconciled and all things promise peace. The darkness is dispell'd and drooping nature revives at the approaching dawn. Look back Oh! my soul, look back and tremble. Rejoice at thy deliverance, and humble thyself in the presence of thy deliverer.

Yet hold, Oh vain mortal! Check thy ill timed joy. Art thou so selfish to exult because thy lot is happy in a season of universal woe? Hast thou no feelings for the miseries of thy fellow-creatures? And art thou incapable of the soft pangs of sympathetic sorrow? Look around

The logo of St. Croix's
English-language newspaper

ALL: THE ROYAL LIBRARY, COPENHAGEN

A nineteenth-century woodcut
shows a hurricane striking the
harbor of the island of St. Thomas.

thee and shudder at the view. See desolation and ruin where'er thou turnest thine eye! See thy fellow-creatures pale and lifeless; their bodies mangled, their souls snatched into eternity, unexpecting. Alas! perhaps unprepared! Hark the bitter groans of distress. See sickness and infirmities exposed to the inclemencies of wind and water! See tender infancy pinched with hunger and hanging on the mothers knee for food! See the unhappy mothers anxiety. Her poverty denies relief, her breast heaves with pangs of maternal pity, her heart is bursting, the tears gush down her cheeks. Oh sights of woe! Oh distress unspeakable! My heart bleeds, but I have no power to solace! O ye, who revel in affluence, see the afflictions of humanity and bestow your superfluity to ease them. Say not, we have suffered also, and thence withold your compassion. What are your sufferings compared to those? Ye have still more than enough left. Act wisely. Succour the miserable and lay up a treasure in Heaven.

I am afraid, Sir, you will think this description more the effort of imagination than a true picture of realities. But I can affirm with the greatest truth, that there is not a single circumstance touched upon, which I have not absolutely been an eye witness to.

Our General [Ulrich Wilhelm Roepstorff, Governor General of St. Croix] has issued several very salutary and humane regulations, and both in his publick and private measures, has shewn himself *the Man*.

Just Published
And to be sold by the Printer hereof
A SERMON,
By the Rev. HUGH KNOX, on occasion of the late Storm—*Price 6 Old Bitts.*
Also Ditto's Discourses in two Volumes, neatly bound—*Ps. 2. 4. Reals.*
Also Ditto's Printed Letter, to the Rev. Mr. Green—*Price Rx. 1.*
Also other single Sermons by ditto—*Price 6 Old Bitts.*

The Reverend Hugh Knox published his own thoughts on the hurricane.

Impressed by Hamilton's obvious intelligence and talents, several wealthy residents of St. Croix subscribed to a fund for the young man's education. Soon after his account of the hurricane was published, Hamilton sailed for North America, where friends of Nicholas Cruger and his family could look out for his welfare and arrange for his schooling. First, Hamilton spent a year in New Jersey, where he received private tutoring that prepared him for admission to college. During this period, he lived in the homes of men like Elias Boudinot, a kindly lawyer who remained Hamilton's lifelong friend. For Hamilton, who had had no home or family of his own since his mother's death, the year in New Jersey was a heart-warming experience. In 1774, after he entered King's College (now Columbia University) in New York, Hamilton expressed some of his feelings for the Boudinots in a poem written to commemorate the death of their daughter Maria.

[New York, September 4, 1774]

For the sweet babe, my doating heart
Did all a Mother's fondness feel;
Carefull to act each tender part
and guard from every threatening ill.

But alass! availd my care?
The unrelenting hand of death,
Regardless of a parent's prayr
Has stoped my lovely Infant's breath—

With rapture number Oer thy Charms,
While on thy harmless sports intent,
Or pratling in my happy arms—

No more thy self Important tale
Some embryo meaning shall convey,
Which should th' imperfect accents fail,
Thy speaking looks would still display—

Thou'st gone, forever gone—yet where,
Ah! pleasing thought; to endless bliss.
Then, why Indulge the rising tear?
Canst thou, fond heart, lament for this?

Let reason silence nature's strife,
And weep Maria's fate no more;
She's safe from all the storms of life,
And Wafted to a peacefull Shore.

Elias Boudinot

In the winter of 1774, there were many distractions for undergraduates at King's College. New York politics had always been characterized by battles in the columns of local newspapers and skirmishes with handbills and pamphlets, and a new war of words was erupting over the growing anti-imperial movement. In September, the First Continental Congress had assembled in Philadelphia to consider the effects of the "Intolerable Acts," by which the British Parliament hoped to stifle Colonial protests. To implement their opposition to British policies, the congressmen adopted measures for economic retaliation—creating a "Continental Association," which decreed nonimportation and nonconsumption of British goods.

Loyalist opposition to the Congress and its Association found a spokesman in the New York press when "A Westchester Farmer" began his attacks on Congress in local newspapers in November, 1774. A month later, readers were introduced to a new political analyst, "A Friend to America," who published "A Full Vindication of the Measures of the Congress" in reply to the Farmer's criticisms. In reality, the "Friend to America" was Hamilton, and his article of December 15, 1774, showed how quickly he had mastered the issues in the Colonial dispute and how well he had learned the arguments that would further the Whig cause.

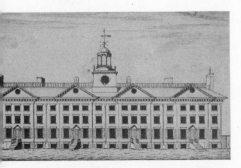

A view of Columbia College, 1790

The Reverend Samuel Seabury,
author of the Loyalist essays
signed by "A Westchester Farmer"

New-York [December 15] 1774
And first, let me ask these restless spirits, whence arises that violent antipathy they seem to entertain, not only to the natural rights of mankind; but to common sense and common modesty. That they are enemies to the natural rights of mankind is manifest, because they wish to see one part of their species enslaved by another. That they have an invincible aversion to common sense is apparent in many respects: They endeavour to persuade us, that the absolute sovereignty of parliament does not imply our absolute slavery; that it is a Christian duty to submit to be plundered of all we have, merely because some of our fellow-subjects are wicked enough to require it of us, that slavery, so far from being a great evil, is a great blessing; and even, that our contest with Britain is founded entirely upon the petty duty of 3 pence per pound on East India tea; whereas the whole world knows, it is built upon this interesting question, whether the inhabitants of Great-Britain have a right to dispose of the lives and properties of the inhabitants of America, or not? And lastly, that these men have discarded all pretension to common modesty, is clear from hence, first, because they, in the plainest terms, call an august body of men, famed for their patriotism and abilities, fools or knaves, and of course the people whom they represented cannot be exempt from the same opprobrious appellations; and secondly, because they set themselves up as standards of wisdom and probity, by contradicting and censuring the public voice in favour of those men. . . .

[Hamilton's "Vindication" then went on to prove that enslavement of the American Colonies was inevitable unless British policies were reversed.]

The only distinction between freedom and slavery consists in this: In the former state, a man is governed by the laws to which he has given his consent, either in person, or by his representative: In the latter, he is governed by the will of another. In the one case his life and property are his own, in the other, they depend upon the pleasure of a master. It is easy to discern which of these two states is preferable. No man in his senses can hesitate in choosing to be free, rather than a slave.

That Americans are intitled to freedom, is incontestible upon every rational principle. All men have one common original: they participate in one common nature, and consequently have one common right. No reason can be assigned why one man should exercise any power, or pre-eminence over his fellow creatures more than another; unless they have voluntarily vested him with it. Since then, Americans have not by any act of their's impowered the British Parliament to make laws for them, it follows they can have no just authority to do it.

Besides the clear voice of natural justice in this respect, the fundamental principles of the English constitution are in our favour. It has been repeatedly demonstrated, that the idea of legislation, or taxation, when the subject is not represented, is inconsistent with *that*. Nor is this all, our charters, the express conditions on which our progenitors relinquished their native countries, and came to settle in this, preclude every claim of ruling and taxing us without our assent. . . .

What then is the subject of our controversy with the mother country? It is this, whether we shall preserve that security to our lives and properties, which the law of nature, the genius of the British constitution, and our charters afford us; or whether we shall resign them into the hands of the British House of Commons, which is no more privileged to dispose of them than the Grand Mogul? What can actuate those men, who labour to delude any of us into an opinion, that the object of contention between the parent state and the colonies is only three pence duty upon tea? or that the commotions in America originate in a plan, formed by some turbulent men to erect it into a republican government? . . .

[The Farmer had argued that Americans should confine themselves to petitioning the Crown, not electing congresses or threatening Britain with economic retaliation, but Hamilton contended that only these stronger measures could impress King and Parliament.]

The only scheme of opposition, suggested by those, who

A contemporary wash drawing of the Boston Tea Party

have been, are averse from a non-importation and non-exportation agreement is, by REMONSTRANCE and PETITION. The authors and abettors of this scheme, have never been able to *invent* a single argument to prove the likelihood of its succeeding. On the other hand, there are many standing facts, and valid considerations against it.

In the infancy of the present dispute, we had recourse to this method only. We addressed the throne in the most loyal and respectful manner...but...our address was treated with contempt and neglect. The first American congress did the same, and met with similar treatment....

There is less reason now than ever to expect deliverance, in this way, from the hand of oppression. The system of slavery, fabricated against America, cannot at this time be considered as the effect of inconsideration and rashness. It is the offspring of mature deliberation. It has been fostered by time, and strengthened by every artifice human subtilty is capable of....

This being the case, we can have no resource but in a restriction of our trade, or in a resistance *vi & armis*. It is impossible to conceive any other alternative. Our congress, therefore, have imposed what restraint they thought necessary. Those, who condemn or clamour against it, do nothing more, nor less, than advise us to be slaves....

[Even more important, Hamilton had to prove to Americans that nonimportation would work—that the "inconveniencies" of doing without British goods for a few months would be balanced by swift changes in British policies.]

No person, that has enjoyed the sweets of liberty, can be insensible of its infinite value, or can reflect on its reverse, without horror and detestation. No person, that is not lost to every generous feeling of humanity, or that is not stupidly blind to his own interest, could bear to offer himself and posterity as victims at the shrine of despotism, in preference to enduring the short lived inconveniencies that may result from an abridgment, or even entire suspension of commerce....

The evils which may flow from the execution of our measures, if we consider them with respect to their extent and duration, are comparatively nothing. In all human probability they will scarcely be felt. Reason and

experience teach us, that the consequences would be too
fatal to Great Britain to admit of delay. There is an immense trade between her and the colonies.... The experiment we have made heretofore, shews us of how
much importance our commercial connexion is to her;
and gives us the highest assurance of obtaining immediate redress by suspending it.

From these considerations it is evident, she must do
something decisive. She must either listen to our complaints, and restore us to a peaceful enjoyment of our
violated rights; or she must exert herself to enforce her
despotic claims by fire and sword. To imagine she would
prefer the latter, implies a charge of the grossest infatuation of madness itself....

[While his "Vindication" met the general arguments
against Congress's Association, Hamilton realized that
he must speak directly to one specific group, the farmers
of New York, whom Loyalists hoped to win over by declaring that nonimportation was merely a scheme to enrich
merchants and townspeople. In a postscript to his "Vindication," Hamilton skillfully played on local pride,
making a special "Address" to the Colony's shrewd, independent rural citizens.]

The reason I address myself to you, in particular, is,
[not] because I am one of your number, or connected
with you in interest more than with any other branch of
the community. I love to speak the truth, and would scorn
to prejudice you in favour of what I have to say, by taking
upon me a fictitious character as other people have done.
I can venture to assure you, the true writer of the piece
signed by A. W. FARMER, is not in reality a Farmer. He
is some ministerial emissary, that has assumed the name
to deceive you, and make you swallow the intoxicating
potion he has prepared for you. But I have a better opinion of you than to think he will be able to succeed. I am
persuaded you love yourselves and children better than
to let any designing men cheat you out of your liberty
and property, to serve their own purposes. You would be
a disgrace to your ancestors, and the bitterst enemies to
yourselves and to your posterity, if you did not act like
men, in protecting and defending those rights you have
hitherto enjoyed....

An English cartoon of 1773 contrasts Britain's prosperity under George II and George III.

[Having described the economic consequences of non-importation for New Yorkers, Hamilton appealed to the farmers' pride and dislike of authority.]

Are you willing then to be slaves without a single struggle? Will you give up your freedom, or, which is the same thing, will you resign all security for your life and property, rather than endure some small present inconveniencies? Will you not take a little trouble to transmit the advantages you now possess to those, who are to come after you? I cannot doubt it. I would not suspect you of so much baseness and stupidity, as to suppose the contrary.

Pray who can tell me why a farmer in America is not as honest and good a man, as a farmer in England? or why has not the one as good a right to what he has earned by his labour, as the other? I can't, for my life, see any distinction between them. And yet it seems the English farmers are to be governed and taxed by their own Assembly, or Parliament; and the American farmers are not.... The latter are to be loaded with taxes by men three thousand miles off; by men, who have no interest, or connexions among them; but whose interest it will be to burden them as much as possible; and over whom they cannot have the least restraint. How do you like this doctrine my friends? Are you ready to own the English farmers for your masters? Are you willing to acknowledge their right to take your property from you, [how] and when they please? I know you scorn the thought....

The Farmer cries, "tell me not of delegates, congresses committees, mobs, riots, insurrections, associations; a plague on them all. Give me the steady, uniform, unbiassed influence of the courts of justice. I have been happy under their protection, and I trust in God, I shall be so again."

I say, tell me not of the British Commons, Lords, ministry, ministerial tools, placemen, pensioners, parasites. I scorn to let my life and property depend upon the pleasure of any of them. Give me the steady, uniform, unshaken security of constitutional freedom; give me the right to be tried by a jury of my own neighbours, and to be taxed by my own representatives only....

[In summarizing his "Address" to the farmers of the

29

province, Hamilton deftly pictured the Westchester Farmer as a British agent who secretly despised the very people to whom he had appealed.]

Will you then, my friends, allow yourselves, to be duped by this artful enemy? will you follow his advices, disregard the authority of your congress, and bring ruin on yourselves and posterity? will you act in such a manner as to deserve the hatred and resentment of all the rest of America? I am sure you will not. I should be sorry to think, any of my countrymen would be so mean, so blind to their own interest, so lost to every generous and manly feeling.

The sort of men I am opposing give you fair words, to persuade you to serve their own turns; but they think and speak of you in common in a very disrespectful manner. I have heard some of their party talk of you, as the most ignorant and mean-spirited set of people in the world. They say, that you have no sense of honour or generosity ... and that you are so ignorant, as not to be able to look beyond the present; so that if you can once be persuaded to believe the measures of your congress will involve you in some little present perplexities, you will be glad to do anything to avoid them; without considering the much greater miseries that await you at a little distance off.... I flatter myself you will convince them of their error, by shewing the world, you are capable of judging what is right and [best], and have resolution to pursue it.

All I ask is, that you will judge for yourselves. I don't desire you to take my opinion or any man's opinion, as the guide of your actions. I have stated a number of plain arguments; I have supported them with several well-known facts: It is your business to draw a conclusion and act accordingly.

I caution you, again and again, to beware of the men who advise you to forsake the plain path, marked out for you by the congress. They only mean to deceive and betray you.... If you join with the rest of America in the same common measure, you will be sure to preserve your liberties inviolate; but if you separate from them, and seek for redress alone, and unseconded, you will certainly fall a prey to your enemies, and repent your folly as long as you live.

(Text continued on page 42)

THE
CONGRESS
CANVASSED:
OR
An EXAMINATION
INTO
The Conduct of the Delegates,
AT THEIR
GRAND CONVENTION,
Held in Philadelphia, Sept. 1, 1774.
ADDRESSED,
To the MERCHANTS of New-York.

By *A.W.* Farmer.
Author of Free Thoughts, *&c.*

Hæc, per Deos immortales, utrum esse vobis consilia siccorum, an vinolentorum somnia? Et utrum cogitata sapientum, an optata furiosorum, videntur? Cicer. contra Rullum.

Do you look upon these Proceedings as the Counsels of Sobriety, or the Dreams of Inebriation? Do they seem to you the Deliberations of Wisdom, or the Ravings of Phrenzy?

PRINTED IN THE YEAR M,DCC,LXXIV.

Title page, 1774, of the attack on Congress by "A Westchester Farmer"

An Ambitious Young Man

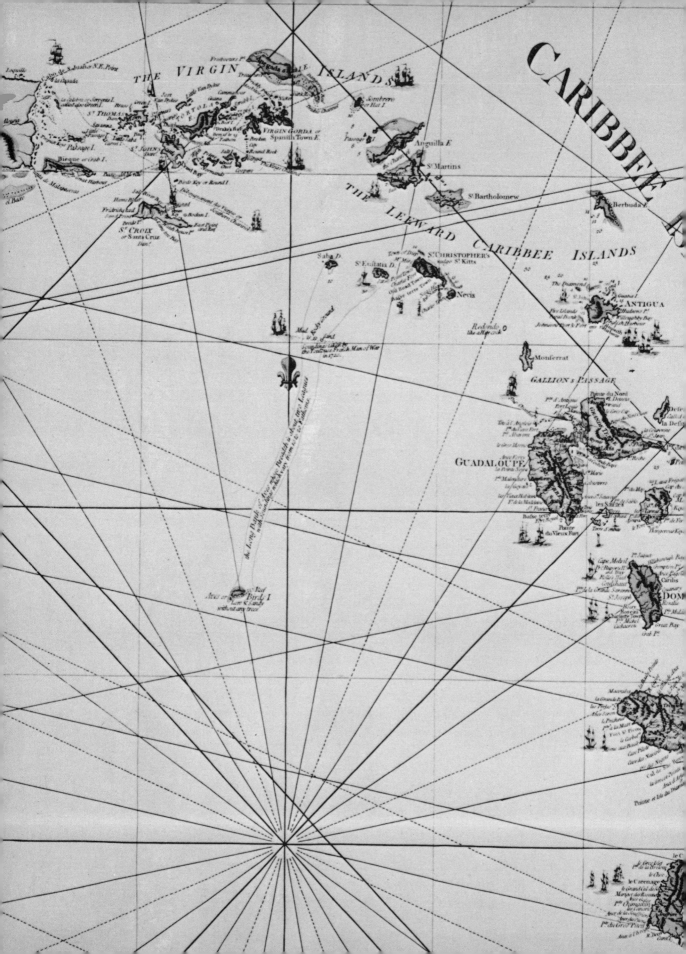

CARIBBEAN BOYHOOD

For many, life on a Caribbean island in the eighteenth century could be extremely pleasant. Residing in great houses and surrounded by outbuildings for their managers and slaves, the owners of a typical plantation such as Prosperity (above) on St. Croix made a comfortable living off the main crop of sugar cane. Their mills (one can be seen in the center of the water color) processed the cane into sugar and rum, both commodities much in demand by the world far from their sunny shores. For young Alexander Hamilton, however, life was a series of hurdles to be overcome. The "bastard brat of a Scotch pedlar," as John Adams was later to call him, Hamilton is thought to have been born in January, 1755, on the tiny British island of Nevis (under the word "Leeward" on the map at left). Illegitimacy, abandonment, poverty, and tragic loss marked the early years of the highly intelligent boy and undoubtedly did much to supply the urgent drive that characterized his later career.

MERCHANT'S APPRENTICE

Christiansted, the main port of St. Croix, was a beehive of trading activity in Hamilton's day. It is pictured below as it appeared from the harbor at that time, and at right in a view looking from the town out to the bay. Young Alexander was apprenticed to Nicholas Cruger (below, far right), whose place of business was located on the lower end of King Street (the colonnaded buildings leading directly to the wharves in the water color at right). Cruger dealt in a variety of merchandise, as his advertisements in the local paper (below, right) indicate. Hamilton kept Cruger's books and wrote many of his letters, and when his employer went to America in 1771, sixteen-year-old Alexander was left in charge. A measure of his application to the job can be seen in a progress report to Cruger: "Believe me Sir I dun as hard as is proper."

Juft Imported, and to be fold

By Nicholas Cruger,

SUPERfine and Common Philadelphia Flour,
Do. Do. New-York Do.
Rye Do.
Shipbread in tierces and barrels,
Kegs Water Bread,
Corn in hhds.
Dry Codfiſh in bbls.
Pickled Fiſh in bbls.
Burlington Pork,
Hams,
New Iriſh Butter,
Oats in hhds. and by the buſhel,
Tobacco in hhds.
Bohea and Congo Tea in cheſts and canniſters,
Madeira Wine in pipes,
White Pine Albany plar.k,
Georgia Pitch Pine Joiſt,
Scantling and Shingles,
White Oak Staves and Heading,
Red Oak do.
Lime in hhds.
Sailduck,
White Lead and Yellow Oaker ground in oil,
Nails and Brads of diff.rent ſorts,
HL Hinges, Hooks, Fenders & Stags for Spouts,
A parcel of ſeaſoned Main & Porto-Rico Mules.
Do. of Draught Cattle.
St. Croix, December 4, 1773.

Juſt imported from the Windward Coaſt of A-
FRICA, and to be ſold on Monday next, by
Meſſrs. Kortright & Cruger,
At ſaid CRUGER's Yard,
Three Hundred Prime
S L A V E S.
⁂ The terms will be made known at the
place of ſale.
Jan. 23, 1771.

BLOWN INTO HISTORY

The otherwise idyllic Caribbean islands are subject to frequent hurricanes. In 1772, a disastrous storm sweeping over St. Croix made such a vivid impression on Hamilton that he wrote a long letter to his father, then living on St. Vincent Island, describing its horrors. Although the aquatint at left depicts the devastation of another of the Virgin Islands after a hurricane, the effect on St. Croix was much the same—five hundred buildings, including Cruger's store, were damaged or destroyed. A minister named Hugh Knox saw the youth's letter and had it published in the *Royal Danish-American Gazette* (logo, above), where it received considerable acclaim. Through Knox's efforts, combined with Cruger's New York contacts, it was arranged for Hamilton to go north to college. The ambitious young man was on his way, thanks to a hurricane that has been aptly described as having "blown Alexander Hamilton into history."

DANISH MARITIME MUSEUM, KRONBORG CASTLE, HELSINGOR

CONFIDENT SCHOLAR

Armed with letters of credit through the generosity of Cruger, young Hamilton
headed in 1773 for Elizabethtown, New Jersey, where Hugh Knox had arranged for
him to prepare for college. Because Hamilton in characteristic fashion wanted
to follow a course of independent study, Princeton turned him down. King's
College in New York, now known as Columbia University (seen above as it looked
when Hamilton first saw it), agreed to take him on his own terms. The matricula
of 1774 (right) has Alexander Hamilton's name second from the bottom, though it
is possible he was admitted a year earlier. His responsibilities during his formative
years with Cruger's firm stood him in good stead; he arrived on the mainland with
a businessman's knowledge of American commerce. Not yet twenty but confident
and ambitious, he met New York head on and soon began to make himself known
in the northern metropolis.

Admissions Anno 1774.

David Clarkson.
Schuyler Lupton.
Jacob Shaw.
John Gaine.
John Whitaker. Left College 3d Year
Samuel Deall.
Horatio Smith.
Paul Randall.
John Brickell.
David Moore.
Edward Cornwallis Winceislee. Up College 2d Year
James Stiles. Left the College in the 2d Year
James Depeyster.
Tristim Lowther.
Thomas Attwood.
Alexander Hamilton.

Nicholas Romeyn S.M.

IMPASSIONED PAMPHLETEER

At college Hamilton joined a student literary society and closely followed the pamphlet war that was raging in the Thirteen Colonies. Even at the tender age of ten, he had been made aware of the controversial Stamp Act when boatloads of men from the neighboring island of St. Kitts had come to Nevis to help destroy the stamped papers. Most of the men he first met in America were patriots, Colonial residents with strong grievances against the mother country, and Hamilton soon joined their ranks as a pamphleteer of considerable talents. His first effort (right) was in answer to a Loyalist pamphlet that had appeared in November of 1774, just three weeks after the Continental Congress had adjourned. Hamilton, however, was apparently opposed to violence, and when a group of angry New Yorkers threatened to attack the home of Myles Cooper, the Loyalist president of King's College (below), it was Hamilton—according to a popular but unsubstantiated legend—who stood in the doorway and talked eloquently to the mob long enough to allow Cooper to escape out the back door.

A
FULL VINDICATION
OF THE
Meafures of the Congrefs,
FROM

The CALUMNIES of their ENEMIES;

IN ANSWER to

A LETTER,

Under the Signature of

A. W. FARMER.

WHEREBY

His *Sophiftry* is expofed, his *Cavils* confuted, his *Artifices* detected, and his *Wit* ridiculed;

IN

A GENERAL ADDRESS

To the Inhabitants of America,

AND

A Particular Addrefs

To the FARMERS *of the Province of New-York.*

by Alexander Hamilton.

Veritas magna eft & prævalebit.
Truth is powerful, and will prevail.

N E W - Y O R K:
Printed by JAMES RIVINGTON. 1774.

(Text continued from page 30)

May God give you wisdom to see what is your true interest, and inspire you with becoming zeal for the cause of virtue and mankind.

A FRIEND TO AMERICA.

Within a few weeks of the publication of Hamilton's "Vindication" of the Continental Association, the Westchester Farmer made a counterattack in his "View of the Controversy Between Great-Britain and her Colonies." Using his pseudonym of "A Friend to America," Hamilton renewed his fight and replied with a lengthy pamphlet dated February 23, 1775. This piece, "The Farmer Refuted: or A more impartial and comprehensive View of the Dispute...," summarized Hamilton's position on the tragic controversy that threatened the Empire.

New-York [February 23, 1775]
Whatever opinion may be entertained of my sentiments and intentions, I attest that being, whose all-seeing eye penetrates the inmost recesses of the heart, that I am not influenced (in the part I take) by any unworthy motive—that, if I am in an error, it is my judgment, not my heart, that errs. That I earnestly lament the unnatural quarrel, between the parent state and the colonies; and most ardently wish for a speedy reconciliation, a perpetual and *mutually* beneficial union, that I am a warm advocate for limited monarchy and an unfeigned well-wisher to the present Royal Family.

But on the other hand, I am inviolably attached to the essential rights of mankind, and the true interests of society. I consider civil liberty, in a genuine unadulterated sense, as the greatest of terrestrial blessings. I am convinced, that the whole human race is intitled to it; and, that it can be wrested from no part of them, without the blackest and most aggravated guilt.

I verily believe also, that the best way to secure a permanent and happy union, between Great-Britain and the colonies, is to permit the latter to be as free, as they desire. To abridge their liberties, or to exercise any power over them, which they are unwilling to submit to, would be a perpetual source of discontent and animosity. A continual jealousy would exist on both sides. This would lead to tyranny, on the one hand, and to sedition and rebellion, on the other. Impositions, not really grievous in themselves, would be thought so; and the murmurs

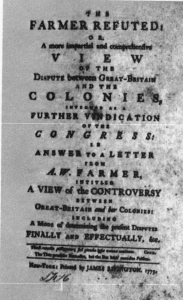

The title page of Hamilton's 1775 pamphlet "The Farmer Refuted"

arising from thence, would be considered as the effect of a turbulent ungovernable spirit. These jarring principles would, at length, throw all things into disorder; and be productive of an irreparable breach, and a total disunion.

That harmony and mutual confidence may speedily be restored, between all the parts of the British empire, is the favourite wish of one, who feels the warmest sentiments of good will to mankind, who bears no enmity to you, and who is,

A SINCERE FRIEND TO AMERICA.

Within a few months the nature of the controversy disputed by Hamilton and the Westchester Farmer had changed drastically. In December, 1774, Hamilton had declared that it would be "the grossest infatuation of madness itself" for Britain to "enforce her despotic claims by fire and sword," but the skirmishes at Lexington and Concord in April, 1775, showed that such "madness" was now a reality. Accordingly, Hamilton took a much harder line in his next publication, "Remarks on the Quebec Bill." The bill, passed by the British Government in 1774, provided for the protection of the Catholic Church and for the administration of French law and judicial practice in the French-Canadian provinces that Britain had won in the French and Indian War a decade earlier. But Protestants in neighboring Colonies saw these provisions as a threat to their own religious freedom.

[New York, June 15, 1775]

Therefore it is apparent, that a system of French laws has been re-established, in the province of Quebec, and an indefinite power vested in the King, to vary and alter those laws, as also to constitute such courts of criminal civil and ecclesiastical jurisdiction, and to introduce such a form of criminal law, as he shall judge necessary; I say since all this is deducible, from the express letter of the act; or in other words, since the whole legislative, executive, and judiciary powers are ultimately and effectually, though not immediately, lodged in the King, there can be no room to doubt, that an arbitrary government has been really instituted throughout the extensive region now comprised in the province of Quebec.

In Part Two of his "Remarks," Hamilton discussed Britain's new toleration of Catholicism in Canada and warned Americans to take care lest their own freedom be destroyed by this British "plot."

In this English comment on the Quebec Act, a bishop is prevented from landing in America.

[New York, June 22, 1775]

Had there been really provision made, to be applied at the discretion of his Majesty, I should still consider this act as an atrocious infraction on the rights of Englishmen, in a point of the most delicate and momentous concern. No protestant Englishman would consent to let the free exercise of his religion depend upon the mere pleasure of any man, however great or exalted. The privilege of worshipping the deity in the manner his conscience dictates, which is one of the dearest he enjoys, must in that case be rendered insecure and precarious. Yet this is the unhappy situation, to which the protestant inhabitants of Canada are now reduced. The will of the King must give law to their consciences. It is in his power to keep them for ever dispossessed of all religious immunities; and there is too much reason to apprehend, that the same motives which instigated the act, would induce him to give them as little future encouragement as possible. . . .

This act develops the dark designs of the ministry more fully than any thing they have done; and shews, that they have formed a systematic project of absolute power. The present policy of it is evidently this. By giving a legal sanction to the accustomed dues of the priests, it was intended to interest them in behalf of administration; and by means of the dominion they possess over the minds of the laity, together with the appearance of good will towards their religion, to prevent any dissatisfaction, which might arise from the loss of their civil rights, and to propitiate them to the great purposes in contemplation; first the subjugation of the colonies and afterwards that of Britain itself. . . .

What can speak in plainer language, the corruption of the British Parliament, than its act; which invests the King with absolute power over a little world . . . and makes such ample provision for the popish religion, and leaves the protestant, in such dependent disadvantageous situation that he is like to have no other subjects, in this part of his domain, than Roman catholics; who, by reason of their implicit devotion to their priests, and the superlative reverence they bear to those, who countenance and favour their religion, will be the voluntary instruments of ambition; and will be ready, at all times, to second the oppressive designs of administration against

44

the other parts of the empire.

Hence...it behoves us to be upon our guard against the deceitful wiles of those, who would persuade us, that we have nothing to fear from the operation of the Quebec act. We should consider it as being replete with danger, to ourselves, and as threatening ruin to our posterity. Let us not therefore suffer ourselves to be terrified at the prospect of an imaginary and fictitious Sylla, and, by that means, be led blindfold into a real and destructive Charybdis.

In the months that followed the publication of his "Remarks on the Quebec Bill," Hamilton was an unhappy observer of the methods used by some men to defend America's liberties. He himself had already faced mob violence in May, 1775, when he protected Myles Cooper, the Tory president of King's College, from a group of angry New Yorkers. Such vigilante action increased in the city and on November 20, a leader of the Sons of Liberty named Isaac Sears took a band of followers across the border from Connecticut into Westchester County and Manhattan to seize New York Loyalists. On November 23, they destroyed the printing presses of James Rivington, the leading Tory newspaperman in New York City, and carried some of his equipment back to Connecticut. Alarmed by these acts, Hamilton wrote to John Jay, one of New York's delegates to the Continental Congress, to report on the situation and to suggest legislation that would discourage such raids in the future.

New York Novem 26. 1775

Though I am fully sensible how dangerous and pernicious Rivington's press has been, and how detestable the character of the man is in every respect, yet I cannot help disapproving and condemning this step.

In times of such commotion as the present, while the passions of men are worked up to an uncommon pitch there is great danger of fatal extremes. The same state of the passions which fits the multitude, who have not a sufficient stock of reason and knowlege to guide them, for opposition to tyranny and oppression, very naturally leads them to a contempt and disregard of all authority. The due medium is hardly to be found among the more intelligent, it is almost impossible among the unthinking populace. When the minds of these are loosened from their attachment to ancient establishments and courses, they seem to grow giddy and are apt more or less to run into anarchy. These principles, too true in themselves, and confirmed to me both by reading and my own experience, deserve extremely the attention of those, who have the direction of public affairs. In such tempestuous times, it requires the greatest skill in the political pilots to keep men steady and within proper bounds, on which account I am always more or less alarmed at every thing which is done of mere will and pleasure, without any proper authority. Irregularities I know are to be expected, but they are nevertheless dangerous and ought to be checked, by every prudent and moderate mean. From these general maxims, I disapprove of the irruption in question, as serving to cherish a spirit of disorder at a season when men are too prone to it of themselves....

[Quite aside from general principles of justice and law and order, Hamilton pointed out, there were several very practical reasons for putting an end to such highhanded actions by New England radicals.]

Antipathies and prejudices have long subsisted between this province and New England. To this may be attributed a principal part of the disaffection now prevalent among us. Measures of the present nature, however they may serve to intimidate, will secretly revive and increase those ancient animosities, which though smothered for a while will break out when there is a favorable opportunity.

Besides this, men coming from a neighbouring province to chastise the notorious friends of the ministry here, will hold up an idea to our ennemies not very advantageous to our affairs. They will imagine that the New Yorkers are totally, or a majority of them, disaffected to the American cause, which makes the interposal of their neighbours necessary: or that such violences will breed differences and effect that which they have been so eagerly wishing, a division and quarrelling among ourselves. Every thing of such an aspect must encourage their hopes.

Upon the whole the measure is condemned, by all the cautious and prudent among the whigs, and will evidently be productive of secret jealousy and ill blood if a stop is not put to things of the kind for the future.

All the good purposes that could be expected from such

James Rivington

a step will be answered; and many ill consequences will be prevented if your body gently interposes a check for the future.... Believe me sir it is a matter of consequence and deserves serious attention.

The tories it is objected by some are growing insolent and clamorous: It is necessary to repress and overawe them. There is truth in this; but the present remedy is a bad one. Let your body station in different parts of the province most tainted, with the ministerial infection, a few regiments of troops, raised in Philadelphia the Jerseys or any other province except New England. These will suffice to strengthen and support the Whigs who are still I flatter myself a large majority and to suppress the efforts of the tories. The pretence for this would be plausible. There is no knowing how soon the Ministry may make an attempt upon New York. There is reason to believe they will not be long before they turn their attention to it. In this there will be some order & regularity, and no grounds of alarm to our friends.

I am sir with very great Esteem—Your most hum servant

A. HAMILTON

Encouraged by Jay's response to his letter, Hamilton continued the correspondence. Although he was not yet old enough to vote or hold office, Hamilton was quite ready to give political advice to an older man like Jay, who was a distinguished lawyer ten years his senior. This he did when he learned that local Loyalists had persuaded Governor William Tryon to call for elections for a new provincial assembly in New York. The Tories hoped that a new assembly, recognized by the Crown and dedicated to "constitutional" government, would distract attention from the "illegal" congresses and committees of the disaffected colonists. Hamilton, seeing a way of turning the elections to Whig advantage, outlined his ideas in another letter to Jay.

N York Decemr. 31st. 1775

The tories will be no doubt very artful and intriguing, and it behoves us to be very vigilant and cautious. I have thrown out a hand bill or two to give the necessary alarm, and shall second them by others.

It appears to me that as the best way to keep the attention of the people united and fixed to the same point it would be expedient that four of our Continental delegates should be candidates for this city and county.

47

...The minds of all our friends will naturally tend to these, and the opposition will of course be weak and contemptible, for the whigs I doubt not constitute a large majority of the people. If you approve the hint, I should wish for your presence here. Absence you know is not very favorable to the influence of any person however great.

I shall give you farther notice, as I see the scheme advance to execution.

Governor Tryon called for new assembly elections on January 2, 1776. Two days later, Hamilton wrote to Jay in Philadelphia, urging him to return from the Continental Congress and lead the fight in New York.

A view from Long Island of New York and its harbor in 1776

[New York, January 4, 1776]
You will find by the papers, that a proclamation has been issued for dissolving the old Assembly; writs are making out for the election of a new.

The tories seem to give out that there will be no opposition, but I suspect this as an artifice to throw the people off their guard. I doubt not however the whig Interest will prevail.

I should be glad to see you here with all convenient dispatch; though perhaps your presence may not be absolutely necessary, yet I like not to hazard any thing, or to neglect any step which may have the least tendency to insure success.

Hamilton's political judgment was accurate. But though the Whig slate of delegates to the assembly was elected without opposition in New York City on February 1, 1776, the victory had only symbolic importance. The assembly met briefly on February 14 and adjourned at once, never to convene again. Royal government collapsed, and Governor Tryon retreated to the safety of His Majesty's Ship *Duchess of Gordon*, anchored in New York Harbor. As the spring of 1776 approached, Hamilton, like all New York Whigs, forgot royal assemblies and "constitutional" government and turned his attention to the provincial and continental congresses and the military organizations needed for their defense. New Yorkers knew that they could expect a British invasion of their province as soon as the winter storms ended. Hamilton's youthful wish seemed fulfilled. Although he had come to North America for an education, he had, instead, found a war to insure his fame and "futurity."

Chapter 2

A Soldier's Progress

For a young man with a taste for military glory, there seemed no better place to be than New York in 1776, for in the summer and fall of that year the approach of the British fleet made the city the center of military operations. When the New York congress ordered the recruitment of an artillery company in January, 1776, Alexander Hamilton did not hesitate to volunteer. In March, on the recommendation of an officer and friend, Alexander McDougall, Hamilton was named Captain of the Provincial Company of Artillery.

Hamilton's abilities as a conscientious and businesslike leader were evident from his earliest days of military service. He not only had to recruit and train his own men; he also had to see that they were fed, clothed, and paid. While many young New Yorkers may have fought the enemy as bravely as Hamilton did, few battled the local authorities so stubbornly to provide for their troops. Toward the end of May, 1776, when he learned that his soldiers were not receiving the benefits of a new pay scale, Hamilton sent this indignant letter to the provincial congress.

[New York, May 26, 1776]

I am not personally interested in having an augmentation agreeable to the above rates, because my own pay will remain the same that it now is; but I make this application on behalf of the company, as I am fully convinced such a disadvantageous distinction will have a very pernicious effect on the minds and behaviour of the men. They do the same duty with the other companies and think themselves entitled to the same pay. They have been already comparing accounts and many marks of discontent have lately appeared on this score. As to the circumstance of our being confined to the defence of the Colony, it will have little or no weight, for there are but few in the company who would not as willingly leave the Colony on any necessary expedition as stay in it; and they will not therefore think it reasonable to have their pay curtailed on such a consideration.

At the Battle of Long Island in the last week of August, 1776, the British defeated the American forces and won possession of New York City. It was either during this campaign or in the retreat of Continental troops across New Jersey in the autumn that Washington was struck by Hamilton's abilities and asked him to become his aide-de-camp with the rank of lieutenant colonel in the Continental Army. Although Hamilton had declined a similar appointment to another general's staff, he accepted Washington's offer. He received his new commission on March 1, 1777, and in the weeks that followed he had a brisk introduction to his duties.

But if Hamilton hoped that his new position would bring him military advancement and fame, he soon had reason for doubt. The theater of operations now shifted from New Jersey to Pennsylvania, and although Hamilton was close to the scene of action, he was seldom exposed to fire. More and more Washington began relying on his skills—both as a writer who could draft endless official letters and as a trustworthy officer who could accept responsibility for the uninspiring but necessary tasks of administration. This was not the war of which Hamilton had dreamed in St. Croix, but it was precisely the kind of war to which he was best suited—a war of paperwork and politics, of diplomacy and detail. Writing to his friend Brigadier General Alexander McDougall, Hamilton explained that the general's inquiries about fortifications in New York had gone unanswered because of Washington's illness.

> Head Qrs. Morris Town [New Jersey]
> March 10th. 1777
>
> [His Excellency] has been very much indisposed for three or four days past, insomuch that his attention to business is pronounced by the Doctor to be very improper; and we have made a point of keeping all from him which was not indispensibly necessary. I detained your express a day in hopes of a convenient opportunity to communicate your letter to him; but though he has grown considerably better than he was, I find he is so much pestered with matters, which cannot be avoided, that I am obliged to refrain from troubling him on the occasion; especially as I conceive the only answer he would give, may be given by myself.
>
> It is greatly to be lamented that the present state of things does not admit of having the requisite number of

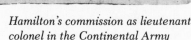

Hamilton's commission as lieutenant colonel in the Continental Army

troops at every post: on the contrary the most important, are deficient. . . . 'Till matters get into a better train, it is impossible but those posts must suffer which, from their situation ought only to be the objects of a secondary attention. We have, I think, the most decisive evidence that the enemy's operations will be directed on this quarter; to this end they are drawing all their forces into the Jerseys, and as soon as the weather will permit 'tis expected they will move towards Philadelphia. Not being very numerous 'tis unlikely they should attempt such an object, without collecting their whole force; and for that reason 'tis not much to be apprehended they should make any stroke of the kind you mention.

Although Hamilton's first loyalties were now to his Commander and to the Continental Army, he did not forget New York or ignore any opportunities to maintain his ties to political leaders in that state. When the Committee of Correspondence of the New York Convention suggested that he furnish them with military news of special interest to their state, Hamilton responded promptly.

[Morristown, New Jersey, March 20, 1777] With chearfulness, I embrace the proposal of corresponding with your convention, through you; and shall from time to time as far as my leisure will permit, and my duty warrant, communicate such [transactions] as shall happen, such pieces of intelligence as shall be received and such comments upon them as shall appear necessary, to convey a true idea of what is going on in the military line. Let me caution you however, that whatever opinions I shall give, in the course of our correspondence, are to be considered merely as my private sentiments; and are never to be interpreted as an echo of those of the *General;* since they will not be really so, and a construction of the kind may lead into errors and be productive of inconveniences.

Pictorial Field-Book of the Revolution
BY BENSON J. LOSSING, 1851

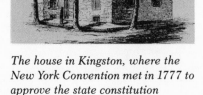

The house in Kingston, where the New York Convention met in 1777 to approve the state constitution

Throughout March, Hamilton assured the New York Committee that the enemy would make "no grand movement" before May, but he soon had to temper his optimism. When the Committee inquired about rumors that the British might advance up the Hudson River, Hamilton admitted that the enemy had moved earlier than expected. But he still contended that Albany was not the primary target.

Head Quarters, Morristown [New Jersey]
April 5th. 1777

The opinion I advanced respecting the Enemy's not moving before the beginning of May seems to be Shaken. ...We have received information that they are embarking about three thousand men on board of transports....

As to your apprehensions of an attempt up the North River I immagine you may discard any uneasiness on that score, though it will be at all times adviseable to be on the watch.... Philadelphia is an object calculated to strike and attract their attention. It has all along been the main source of supplies towards the war and the getting it into their possession would deprive us of a wheel we could very badly spare in the great political and military machine.

Although military affairs grew more serious in May, Hamilton could still devote himself to drafting a lengthy reply to his friend Gouverneur Morris's comments on the new New York constitution. Morris, a member of the state constitutional convention, described the plan as "deficient for the Want of Vigor in the executive unstable from the very Nature of popular elective Governments and dilatory from the Complexity of the Legislature." In mid-May, Hamilton explained his own views of the "frame of government."

Head Quarters Morris Town [New Jersey]
May 19th. 1777

That there is a want of vigor in the executive, I believe will be found true. To determine the qualifications proper for the chief executive Magistrate requires the deliberate wisdom of a select assembly, and cannot be safely lodged with the people at large. That instability is inherent in the nature of popular governments, I think very disputable; unstable democracy, is an epithet frequently in the mouths of politicians; but I believe that from a strict examination of the matter, from the records of history, it will be found that the fluctuation of governments in which the popular principle has borne a considerable sway, has proceeded from its being compounded with other principles and from its being made to operate in an improper channel. Compound governments, though they may be harmonious in the beginning, will introduce distinct interests; and these interests will clash, throw the state into convulsions & produce a change

This elegant Morristown mansion served as Washington's headquarters during the winter of 1779–80.

Revolution, LOSSING

or dissolution. When the deliberative or judicial powers are vested wholly or partly in the collective body of the people, you must expect error, confusion and instability. But a representative democracy, where the right of election is well secured and regulated & the exercise of the legislative, executive and judiciary authorities, is vested in select persons, chosen *really* and not *nominally* by the people, will in my opinion be most likely to be happy, regular and durable. That the complexity of your legislature will occasion delay and dilatoriness is evident and I fear may be attended with much greater evil; as expedition is not very material *in making* laws, especially when the government is well digested and matured by time. The evil I mean is, that in time, your senate, from the very name and from the mere circumstance of its being a separate member of the legislature, will be liable to degenerate into a body purely aristocratical. And I think the danger of an abuse of power from a simple legislative would not be very great, in a government where the equality and fulness of popular representation is so wisely provided for as in yours. On the whole, though I think there are the defects intimated, I think your Government far the best that we have yet seen, and capable of giving long and substantial happiness to the people. Objections to it should be suggested with great caution and reserve.

Pay book of Hamilton's artillery company for August, 1776

While Britain's General William Howe concealed his intentions in the spring of 1777, a young officer in Washington's "family" even had moments for flirtation. During his stay in New Jersey before the Revolution, Alexander Hamilton had become acquainted with the family of William Livingston, the first governor of the state after independence. When Livingston's daughter Catharine asked Hamilton to send her news of the military and political situation, he was only too glad to oblige. He teased Catharine with a lighthearted warning that he would not confine himself to public affairs.

Morris Town [New Jersey] April 11th. 1777
I challenge you to meet me in whatever path you dare; and if you have no objection, for variety and amusement, we will even sometimes make excursions in the flowery walks, and roseate bowers of Cupid. You know, I am renowned for gallantry, and shall always be able to entertain you with a choice collection of the prettiest things

imaginable. I fancy my knowledge of you affords me a tolerably just idea of your taste, but lest I should be mistaken I shall take it kind, if you will give me such intimations of it, as will remove all doubt, and save me the trouble of finding it out with certainty myself....

After knowing exactly your taste, and whether you are of a romantic, or discreet temper, as to love affairs, I will endeavour to regulate myself by it. If you would choose to be a goddess, and to be worshipped as such, I will torture my imagination for the best arguments, the nature of the case will admit, to prove you so. You shall be one of the graces, or Diana, or Venus, or something surpassing them all. And after your deification, I will cull out of every poet of my acquaintance, the choicest delicacies, they possess, as offerings at your Goddesships' shrine. But if, conformable to your usual discernment, you are content with being a mere mortal, and require no other incense, than is justly due to you, I will talk to you like one [in] his sober senses; and, though it may be straining the point a little, I will even stipulate to pay you all the rational tribute properly applicable to a fine girl.

But amidst my amorous transports, let me not forget, that I am also to perform the part of a politician and intelligencer....

Of this, I am pretty confident, that the ensuing campaign will effectually put to death all their hopes; and establish the success of our cause beyond a doubt. You and I, as well as our neighbours, are deeply interested to pray for victory, and its necessary attendant peace; as, among other good effects, they would remove those obstacles, which now lie in the way of that most delectable thing, called matrimony;—a state, which, with a kind of magnetic force, attracts every breast to it, in which sensibility has a place, in spite of the resistance it encounters in the dull admonitions of prudence, which is so prudish and perverse a dame, as to be at perpetual variance with it.

Governor William Livingston

Alexander Hamilton's courtship of "Kitty" Livingston should not be taken too seriously. Five years his senior, Catharine enjoyed flirting and flattery, but cautiously avoided marriage to any of her suitors until 1786. For his part, Hamilton soon had little time for romance, for it was becoming clear that General Howe had an objective in mind. The problem for Washington's headquarters was to sort out the reports of spies, deserters, and prisoners of war to determine what that objective was. By early May, Hamilton had to qualify his confident predictions that the British would turn south, as he warned the New York Committee of Correspondence.

Head Quarters Morris Town [New Jersey]
May 7th. 1777

General William Howe

We have reason to suspect the enemy will soon evacuate Brunswick and push for Amboy; whence they will no doubt embark for some expedition by water...either... to Philadelphia or up the North River....The testimony of every person, that comes from them, confirms this fact, that their horses are in such miserable condition as to render them incapable of any material operations by land. If therefore proper care be taken...to prevent their collecting supplies of good horses among ourselves, I know not how it will be possible for them to penetrate any distance into the Country. As far as it may depend upon them, I hope the Convention will attend to this circumstance & will take effectual measures to put it out of their power to gain such supplies in any part of your state, towards which they may direct their movements.

On May 28, Washington moved his headquarters to Middle Brook, New Jersey, only seven miles from the British post at Brunswick. Middle Brook could be defended easily and was a better point from which to observe Howe's troop movements and to try to figure out his course. For weeks, Howe and Washington played a cat-and-mouse game in New Jersey as the British general tried to draw the Americans away from Middle Brook and the Continental Commander wisely stood his ground. When Howe evacuated Brunswick in the third week of June and withdrew his forces to Amboy, Washington finally ordered his troops into the field. On June 26, Howe moved to cut off the Americans and block their return to the safety of Middle Brook. Although the Continental Army escaped the British trap, Hamilton realized that his Commander would be criticized for choosing to make a timely retreat rather than risk his soldiers in open battle. To prevent such attacks on Washington, Hamilton wrote in confidence to Robert R. Livingston in New York.

Head Quarters Camp at Middle Brook [New Jersey]
June 28 1777

I know the comments that some people will make on our Fabian conduct. It will be imputed either to cowardice or to weakness: But the more discerning, I trust, will not

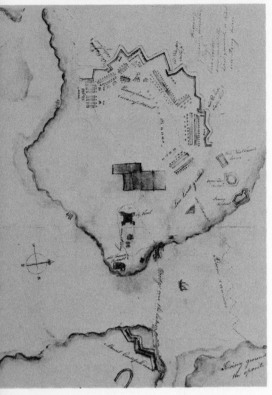

Fort Ticonderoga map by Trumbull

find it difficult to conceive that it proceeds from the truest policy, and is an argument neither of the one nor the other. The liberties of America are an infinite stake. We should not play a desperate game for it or put it upon the issue of a single cast of the die. The loss of one general engagement may effectually ruin us, and it would certainly be folly to hazard it, unless our resources for keeping up an army were at an end, and some decisive blow was absolutely necessary; or unless our strength was so great as to give certainty of success. Neither is the case. America can in all probability maintain its army for years, and our numbers though such as would give a reasonable hope of success are not such as should make us intirely sanguine.... England herself, from the nature of her polity can furnish few soldiers and even these few can ill be spared to come to America in the present hostile appearance of affairs in Europe....

Their affairs will be growing worse—our's better;—so that delay will ruin them. It will serve to perplex and fret them, and precipitate them into measures, that we can turn to good account. Our business then is to avoid a General engagement and waste the enemy away...in a desultory teazing way.

After the engagement of June 26, Howe discarded his plan to lure Washington into open battle in New Jersey and withdrew to Staten Island. In July, headquarters learned that Britain's General John Burgoyne had captured the American post at Fort Ticonderoga in northern New York. Once again, the American command was baffled by British strategy. Believing that Howe might turn north up the Hudson River and join forces with Burgoyne, Washington moved his headquarters to Smiths Clove in Orange County, New York. From there, Hamilton wrote to Gouverneur Morris, vainly trying to understand the curious British movements.

[Smiths Clove, New York, July 22, 1777]

I am doubtful whether Burgoigne will attempt to penetrate far, and whether he will not content himself with harassing our back settlements by parties assisted by the savages.... This doubt arises from some appearances that indicate a Southern movement of General Howes army, which, if it should really happen, will certainly be a barrier against any further impressions of Burgoigne; for it cannot be supposed he would be rash enough to plunge into the bosom of the Country, without an expectation of being met by General Howe.... I confess however that the appearances I allude to do not carry a full evidence in my mind; because ... I cannot conceive upon what principle of common sense or military propriety Howe can be running away from Burgoigne to the Southward.

Luckily, Hamilton's grasp of British military objectives was better than that of Sir William Howe. An administrative comedy of errors destroyed the Crown's carefully laid plans to seize New York and divide the United States. According to a program drawn up in London in March, 1777, General Burgoyne was to march south from Canada to be met at Albany by Howe's forces from southern New York. Howe knew nothing of this plan. Instead, on July 23, he and his army sailed from Staten Island for an attack on Philadelphia. Washington turned his men south to check this move. Not until August 16 did Howe receive orders to capture Philadelphia in time to aid in a "junction" with Burgoyne. Had Howe seen these instructions earlier, or had they been stated more clearly, he could have adjusted his timetable and attempted to move up the Hudson. As it was, reports from the north indicated that Burgoyne was advancing easily through the New York wilderness and was in no need of aid. Indeed, as Hamilton pointed out to Robert R. Livingston, the conduct of New Yorkers indicated that the state might well be frightened into submission.

> Head Quarters Camp
> near German Town [Pennsylvania]
> 7 Augt 1777

> I am with you exceeding anxious for the Safety of your State ... ; the panic in the army (I am afraid pretty high up) and the want of zeal in the Eastern States are the only alarming Considerations, for tho Burgoine should be weak in numbers as I suppose him, if the army Tumble at his name, & those who Command it ready to fly from the most defencible Ground at the Terror of small Scouting Parties of Indians, and, if to Crown the Whole the Eastern States go to Sleep & leave New York dismembered & Exhausted, as it is, to play the whole Game against a Skilfull & Enterprising Antagonist; I say if that is to be the Case, we can look for nothing but Misfortune upon Misfortune, & Conquest without a blow.

On August 22, Howe's fleet was sighted in Chesapeake Bay, and Washington knew, at last, that Philadelphia was the British objective. Marching from Germantown, American forces camped at Wilmington, Delaware. While the British slowly fanned out from their landing point near modern Elkton, Maryland, Hamilton gave Gouverneur Morris yet another report on the puzzling movements of the British commander.

> Head Quarters Wilmington [Delaware]
> September 1st 1777
>
> He still lies there [Greys Hill, Pennsylvania] in a state of inactivity; in a great measure I believe from the want of horses, to transport his baggage and stores. It seems he sailed with only about three weeks provendor and was six at sea. This has occasioned the death of a great number of his horses, and has made skeletons of the rest. He will be obliged to collect a supply from the neighbouring country before he can move....
>
> This Country does not abound in good posts. It is intersected by such an infinity of roads, and is so little mountainous that it is impossible to find a spot not liable to capital defects. The one we now have is all things considered the best we could find, but there is no great depindence to be put upon it. The enemy will have Philadelphia, if they dare make a bold push for it, unless we fight them a pretty general action. I opine we ought to do it, and that we shall beat them soundly if we do. The Militia seem pretty generally stirring. Our army is in high health & spirits. We shall I hope have twice the enemy's numbers. I would not only fight them, but I would attack them; for I hold it an established maxim, that there is three to one in favour of the party attacking.

Hamilton's letter to John Hancock, September 18, 1777, advising Congress to leave Philadelphia

Ten days later, "pretty general action" at Brandywine Creek brought defeat for the Americans. Luckily, Howe did not press his victory, and Washington was able to withdraw in good order. On September 18, Hamilton led a party to destroy flour at Daversers Ferry on the Schuylkill River before Howe's troops could seize these supplies. Early in the day, Hamilton wrote a hurried note to John Hancock, the president of Congress, warning him to leave Philadelphia. Fearing that Hancock might not receive his first message, Hamilton sat down that evening to give him a fuller report on enemy activities.

> [Warwick Furnace, Pennsylvania],
> Sepr. 18th 1777 9 OClock at night
> The enemy are on the road to Sweedes ford [the site of modern Norristown, Pennsylvania], the main body about

The British took refuge from the patriots in the Chew House during the Battle of Germantown.

four miles from it. They sent a party this evening to Davesers ferry, which fired upon me and some others in crossing it, killed one man, wounded another, and disabled my horse. They came on so suddenly that one boat was left adrift on the other side, which will of course fall into their hands and by the help of that they will get possession of another, which was abandonned by those who had the direction of it and left afloat, in spite of every thing that I could do to the contrary. These two boats will convey 50 men across at a time so that in a few hours they may throw over a large party, perhaps sufficient to overmatch the militia who may be between them and the city. This renders the situation of Congress extremely precarious if they are not on their guard; my apprehensions for them are great, though it is not improbable they may not be realized.

Not Washington but Horatio Gates, the commander of the Northern Army, emerged as the hero of the American campaign of 1777. Unable to prevent the British occupation of Philadelphia on September 26, Washington was also defeated at Germantown on October 4. By contrast, Burgoyne surrendered his entire army to Gates at Saratoga on October 17. Although many historians argue that Benedict Arnold deserved the credit for the American success in New York, it was Gates, a man jealous of Washington's power and popularity, who was acclaimed the victor. A few days later Washington and his advisers reached a decision that would bring the rivalry with Gates into the open. Gates was to be asked to send troops from the Northern Army to bolster the American position around Philadelphia. Hamilton was given the thankless assignment of riding to Albany to persuade Gates to part with a "very considerable part of the army at present under his command." On his arrival in Albany on November 5, Hamilton received Gates's promise to release one of the three brigades still at that post. Later in the day, Hamilton complained to Gates that he had been tricked.

Albany [New York], Novemr. 5th. 1777
By inquiry, I have learned that General Patterson's brigade, which is the one you propose to send is, by far, the weakest of the three now here, and does not consist of more than about 600 rank and file fit for duty. It is true there is a militia regiment with it of about 200, but the term of service...is so near expiring, that it would be past by the time the men could arrive at the place of their destination, and to send them would be to fatigue

the men to no purpose. Under these circumstances, I cannot consider it either as compatible with the good of the service or my instructions from His Excellency General Washington, to consent, that that brigade be selected from the three, to go to him; but I am under the necessity of requiring, by virtue of my orders from him, that one of the others be substituted instead of this....

Knowing that General Washington wished me to pay great deference to your judgment, I ventured so far to deviate, from the instructions he gave me as to consent, in compliance with your opinion that two brigades should remain here instead of one....When I preferred your opinion to other considerations, I did not imagine you would pitch upon a brigade little more than half as large as the others; and finding this to be the case I indispensibly owe it to my duty, to desire in His Excellency's name, that another brigade may go instead of the one intended.

Washington's troops waited on the banks of the Brandywine to meet Howe en route to Philadelphia.

The next day, Hamilton reported the touchy situation at Albany to his Commander in Chief.

Albany [New York], November [6] 1777

I felt the importance of strengthening you as much as possible, but on the other hand, I found insuperable inconveniences in acting diametrically opposite to the opinion of a Gentleman, whose successes have raised him into the highest importance. General Gates has won the intire confidence of the Eastern States; if disposed to do it by addressing himself to the prejudices of the people he would find no difficulty to render a measure odious; which it might be said, with plausibility enough to be believed, was calculated to expose them to unnecessary danger, not withstanding their exertions during the campaign had given them the fullest title to repose and security. General Gates has influence and interest elsewhere; he might use it, if he pleased, to discredit the measure there also. On the whole it appeared to me dangerous to insist on sending more troops from hence while General Gates appeared so warmly opposed to it. Should any accident or inconvenience happen in consequence of it, there would be too fair a pretext for censure, and many people are too-well-disposed to lay hold of it. At any rate it might be considered as using him ill to

Hamilton's certification that a man in his artillery company had lost his arm in battle and so was entitled to disability pay

take a step so contrary to his judgment in a case of this nature. These considerations...determined me not to insist upon sending either of the other brigades remaining here. I am afraid what I have done may not meet with your approbation as not being perhaps fully warranted by your instructions; but I ventured to do what I thought right, hoping that at least the goodness of my intention will excuse the error of my judgment.

After Hamilton rejoined the main Army at its new winter headquarters at Valley Forge at the end of December, 1777, he became increasingly concerned over the failure of the Continental Congress to provide for the Army's welfare. While some soldiers struggled to throw up huts in the snow and others froze and starved, Congress seemed more interested in political infighting than in aiding the Army. Moreover, Washington's rivalry with Gates had become a political issue in Congress, and every suggestion of military reform was scrutinized carefully—and slowly. Despairing of prompt action from Congress, Hamilton decided to enlist the aid of George Clinton, New York's newly elected governor, who had proved an invaluable ally in dealing with Gates. Accordingly, he wrote to the governor on "a matter...which requires the attention of every person of sense and influence [: the] degeneracy of representation in the great council of America."

Head Quarters [Valley Forge Pennsylvania]
Feb'y 13. 1778.

General Horatio Gates

It is a melancholy truth Sir, and the effects of which we dayly see and feel, that there is not so much wisdom in a certain body, as there ought to be, and as the success of our affairs absolutely demands. Many members of it are no doubt men in every respect, fit for the trust, but this cannot be said of it as a body. Folly, caprice a want of foresight, comprehension and dignity, characterise the general tenor of their actions. Of this I dare say, you are sensible, though you have not perhaps so many opportunities of knowing it as I have. Their conduct with respect to the army especially is feeble indecisive and improvident—insomuch, that we are reduced to a more terrible situation than you can conceive....

Each State in order to promote its own internal government and prosperity, has selected its best members to fill the offices within itself, and conduct its own affairs. Men have been fonder of the emoluments and conveniences, of being employed at home, and local attachment, falsely operating, has made them more provi-

The War of Independence BY BENSON J. LOSSING, 1850

A nineteenth-century engraving of Washington's camp at Valley Forge during the winter of 1777–78

dent for the particular interests of the states to which they belonged, than for the common interests of the confederacy.... You should not beggar the councils of the United States to enrich the administration of the several members. Realize to yourself the consequences of having a Congress despised at home and abroad. How can the common force be exerted, if the power of collecting it be put in weak foolish and unsteady hands? How can we hope for success in our European negociations, if the nations of Europe have no confidence in the wisdom and vigor, of the great Continental Government?

Late in March, the problem of exchanging prisoners of war with the British became Hamilton's personal concern. Although Howe and Washington had agreed to such an exchange in 1776, arguments over the interpretation of their agreement, and congressional interference, had seriously impeded any exchange. On March 28, 1778, Hamilton and three others were named to a commission to meet with Howe's representatives at Germantown. Their first attempt at negotiation failed, but Hamilton and his colleagues agreed to a second round of talks. That "national character" that Hamilton treasured was threatened again, as the commissioners reported to Washington after their return to Valley Forge.

[Valley Forge, Pennsylvania, April 15, 1778]
[April 7]... The Commissioners... opened [the meeting] by informing us, that [General Howe] meant the Treaty to be of a personal nature, founded on the mutual confidence and honor of the contracting Generals; and had no intention, either of binding the nation, or extending the cartel beyond the limits and duration of his own command....

In answer, we assigned them our reasons at large, for thinking there was a material defect, in their powers, which must render any Treaty, we could form, nugatory and unequal; nugatory, because the private faith of an individual could not in the nature of things be a competent, or proper security for a treaty of public import; and unequal, because, on the one hand, from the express terms of our powers, the public faith would be plighted for our engagements, and on the other, General Howe alone would be bound for the performance of theirs.

The Commissioners from General Howe... intimated an impropriety in treating with us, on a national ground, in a contest of such a nature as the present, which might

Trumbull sketched these starving American prisoners aboard the British prison ship Jersey, *which was anchored in New York Harbor.*

imply an acknowlegement inconsistent with their claims. We observed to them, that if there was any inconsistency at all, it would operate equally against the forming a cartel, on any principle whatever, and against the whole business of exchange;...to remove, as far as was in our power, every impediment to the execution of our commission we proposed, that a clause should be admitted into the cartel, declaring, that no expressions contained in it, should be construed to affect the political claims of either country, in any thing, not directly necessary to the due and faithful observance of the Treaty....

[The British general, however, refused to alter the wording of his commission, and after a brisk exchange of notes and memoranda, the talks ended fruitlessly, as Hamilton and his fellow officers regretfully reported to Washington.]

We are sorry the views of General Sir William Howe were so far different from yours as to render them impracticable. Your powers to us were the standard, by which we were to judge of the sufficiency of his. The former are founded on the broad basis of national faith; the latter, on the narrow one of private faith. A dissimilarity, in so material a point, appeared to us a solid, and on our part, an insuperable objection. We considered the formation of a Treaty, by which such momentous concerns would be affected, with no other sanction, than the personal honor and interest of an individual — not only as incompatible with our commission; but as repugnant to reason, to the nature of the business, and to common usage, in similar cases. A Treaty so formed would, in our conception, be merely nominal, or at best of temporary operation, certainly ceasing with personal command—liable, at any time, to be violated by public authority, without the imputation of public dishonor, and highly derogatory to the dignity of these United States.

After his frustrating negotiations with the British, the summer of 1778 seemed to offer Hamilton his long-awaited chance for military glory. With the news of a Franco-American alliance, General Sir Henry Clinton, Howe's successor as British commander, was ordered to

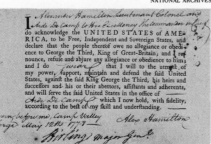

Hamilton's oath of allegiance as aide-de-camp to General Washington

evacuate Philadelphia. Fearful of the arrival of a French fleet, Clinton withdrew his troops overland to New York. On June 19, Washington, with Hamilton at his side, left Valley Forge to pursue the British across New Jersey. Although his advisers urged him to merely harass the British instead of meeting them in open battle, Washington decided on more decisive action. The Marquis de Lafayette and General Anthony Wayne were sent forward, and the Marquis was to engage the enemy as he wished. Assigned to assist Lafayette, Hamilton rode ahead to scout British positions. From a tavern near Allentown, New Jersey, he sent Washington his first bulletin.

Robins Tavern
8 Miles from Allen Town [New Jersey]
12 OClock [June 26, 1778]

The Marquis de Lafayette

Our reason for halting is the extreme distress of the troops for want of provisions. General Wayne's detachment is almost starving and seem both unwilling and unable to march further 'till they are supplied. If we do not receive an immediate supply, the whole purpose of our detachment must be frustrated. This morning we missed doing any thing from a deficiency of intelligence. On my arrival at Cranbury yesterday evening, I proceeded...to take measures for cooperating with the different parts of the detachment and to find what was doing to procure intelligence. I found every precaution was neglected—no horse was near the enemy, or could be heard of 'till late in the morning; so that before we could send out parties and get the necessary information, they were in full march and as they have marched pretty expeditiously we should not be able to come up with them during the march of this day; if we did not suffer the impediment we do on the score of provisions. We are intirely at a loss where the army is, which is no inconsiderable check to our enterprise; if the army is wholly out of supporting distance, we risk the total loss of the detachment in making an attack. If the army will countenance us we may do something clever. We feel our personal honor as well as the honor of the army and the good of the service interested and are heartily desirous to attempt whatever the disposition of our men will second and prudence authorise. It is evident the enemy wish to avoid not to engage us.

Two days later, on the plain near Monmouth Court House, the enemy had no choice but "to engage us." Even then the battle was almost lost because of the indecision of General Charles Lee, Washington's second-in-command. A week after the battle, Hamilton reported on the event to his old friend Elias Boudinot, now a member of Congress. His account began with a denunciation of Lee and the officers who had advised a cautious campaign of harassment.

[New Brunswick, New Jersey
July 5, 1778]

I can hardly persuade myself to be in good humour with success so far inferior to what we, in all probability should have had, had not the finest opportunity America ever possessed been fooled away by a man, in whom she has placed a large share of the most ill judged confidence. You will have heard enough to know, that I mean General Lee. This man is either a driveler in the business of soldiership or something much worse. To let you fully into the silly and pitiful game he has been playing, I will take the tale up from the beginning....

When we came to Hopewell Township, The General unluckily called a council of war, the result of which would have done honor to the most honorab[le] society of midwives, and to them only. The purport was, that we should keep at a comfortable distance from the enemy, and keep up a vain parade of annoying them by detachment. In persuance of this idea, a detachment of 1500 men was sent off under General [Charles] Scot to join the other troops near the enemy's lines. General Lee was *primum mobile* of this sage plan; and was even opposed to sending so considerable a force....

General Charles Lee, by Trumbull

YALE UNIVERSITY ART GALLERY, GIFT OF MRS. ROBERT F. JEFFERYS

[As Hamilton recalled, Lee's behavior became even more erratic when the "advanced corps" under Lafayette was ordered forward on June 25, and became totally incomprehensible when that corps met the enemy on the morning of June 28.]

General Lee's conduct with respect to the command of this corps was truly childish. According to the incorrect notions of our army his seniority would have intitled him to the command of the advanced corps; but he in the first instance declined it, in favour of the Marquis [de Lafayette]. Some of his friends having blamed him for doing it, and Lord Stirling [Major General William Alexander] having shown a disposition to interpose his claim, General Lee very inconsistently reasserted his pretensions. The matter was a second time accommodated; General Lee and Lord Stirling agreed to let the Marquis command. General Lee a little time after, recanted again and became very importunate. The General [Washington], who had all along observed the greatest candor in the matter, grew tired of such fickle behaviour and ordered the Marquis to proceed....

The advanced corps came up with the enemys rear a mile or two beyond the court House; I saw the enemy drawn up, and am persuaded there were not a thousand men; their front from different accounts was then ten miles off. However favourable this situation may seem for an attack it was not made; but after changing their position two or three times by retrograde movements our advanced corps got into a general confused retreat and even route would hardly be too strong an expression. Not a word of all this was officially communicated to the General; as we approached the supposed place of action we heard some flying rumours of what had happened in consequence of which the General rode forward and found the troops retiring in the greatest disorder and the enemy pressing upon their rear. I never saw the general to so much advantage. His coolness and firmness were admirable. He instantly took measures for checking the enemy's advance, and giving time for the army, which was very near, to form and make a proper disposition. He then rode back and had the troops formed on a very advantageous piece of ground; in which and in other transactions of the day General Greene & Lord Stirling rendered very essential service, and did themselves great honor. The sequel is, we beat the enemy and killed and wounded at least a thousand of their best troops. America owes a great deal to General Washington for this day's work; a general route dismay and disgrace would have attended the whole army in any other hands but his. By his own good sense and fortitude he turned the fate of the day.

BOTH: *United States History*, LOSSING

A nineteenth-century engraving of the battleground at Monmouth

The American victory at Monmouth did much to silence Washington's critics in Congress, but another problem rose to plague the Commander's military family. The massive naval aid sent from France proved to be of questionable value. A joint attack on British forces in Rhode Island in August failed when the Count D'Estaing, the French admiral, sailed to Boston to repair his ships rather than remain near Newport to aid Continental troops under generals John Sullivan and Nathanael Greene. After extricating his stranded men, Sullivan was understandably indignant, and openly expressed his doubts as to the value of America's ally in the war against Britain. Early in September, Hamilton explained the situation to Elias Boudinot, pointing out the delicate path that Boudinot and his fellow congressmen would have to take in the matter.

Head Quarters [White Plains, New York]
Sepr 8th. 78.

The military action in Rhode Island, August, 1778

The Frenchmen expect the state will reprobate the conduct of their General, and by that means, make atonement for the stain he has attempted to bring upon French honor. Something of this kind seems necessary and will in all likelihood be expected by the Court of France; but the manner of doing it suggests a question of great delicacy and difficulty, which I find myself unable to solve.

The temper with which General Sullivan was actuated was too analogous to that which appeared in the generality of those concerned with him in the expedition, and to the sentiments prevailing among the people. Though men of discression will feel the impropriety of his conduct; yet there are too many who will be ready to make a common cause with him against any attempt of the public authority to convince him of his presumption, unless the business is managed with great address and circumspection. The credit universally given him for a happy and well conducted retreat, will strengthen the sentiments in his favour, and give an air of cruelty to any species of disgrace, which might be thrown upon a man, who will be thought rather to deserve the esteem and applause of his country. To know how to strike the proper string will require more skill, than I am master of; but I would offer this general hint, that there should be a proper mixture of the *sweet* and *bitter* in the potion which may be administered.

As the campaign of 1778 drew to a close, Hamilton, like the rest of Washington's staff, began to speculate on the enemy's plans for the coming year. It is significant that in discussing this problem in a letter to his friend Alexander McDougall, who was now a major general, Hamilton considered America's economic distress to be as important a factor as military considerations were in determining British policy.

Miniature, by John Ramage, of Major General Alexander McDougall

[Fredericksburg, New York, November 8, 1778] It is a question very undecided in my mind whether the enemy will evacuate or not. Reasoning *a priori* the arguments seem to be strongest for it, from the exhausted state of the British resources, the naked condition of their dominions every where, and the possibility of a Spanish War. But on the other hand naval superiority must do a great deal in the business. This, I think, considering all things appears clearly enough to be on the side of Britain.... The preserving posts in these States will greatly distress our trade and give security to the British West India trade. They will also cover the West Indies, and restrain any operations of ours against the British dominions on the Continent. These considerations and the depreciated state of our currency, will be strong inducements to keep New York and Rhode Island, if not with a view to conquest with a view to temopary advantages, and making better terms in a future negotiation....

The depreciation of our Currency really casts a gloom on our prospects; but my sentiments on this subject are rather peculiar. I think bad as it is, it will continue to draw out the resources of the country a good while longer; and especially if the enemy make such detachments, of which there is hardly a doubt, as will oblige them to act on the defensive. This will make our public expenditure's infinitely less and will allow the states leisure to attend to the arrangement of their finances as well as the country tranquillity to cultivate its resources.

While Hamilton kept in touch with old friends like McDougall, he had also begun to make new friends among Washington's family of junior officers. The closest of these was John Laurens of South Carolina, the son of Henry Laurens, a powerful planter and political figure. A charming, fearless soldier who had served as a volunteer aide to the Commander since 1777, John Laurens had been wounded at Monmouth and had little patience with Charles Lee's attempts to exonerate his own conduct at Washington's expense. Finally, in December, 1778, young Laurens challenged Lee to a duel, and Hamilton, as his friend's second, accompanied him to the edge of a woods near Philadelphia at 3:30 P.M., on December 23. Laurens and Lee chose pistols as weapons and agreed that each was to advance toward the other and fire at will; then the affair of honor began. The next day, Hamilton and Evan Edwards, Lee's second, drew up an official account of the afternoon's events.

[Philadelphia, December 24, 1778]

They approached each other within about five or six paces and exchanged a shot almost at the same moment. As Col Laurens was preparing for a second discharge, General Lee declared himself wounded. Col Laurens, as if apprehending the wound to be more serious than it proved advanced towards the general to offer his support. The same was done by Col Hamilton and Major Edwards under a similar apprehension. General Lee then said the wound was inconsiderable, less than he had imagined at the first stroke of the Ball, and proposed to fire a second time. This was warmly opposed both by Col Hamilton and Major Edwards, who declared it to be their opinion, that the affair should terminate as it then stood. But General Lee repeated his desire, that there should be a second discharge and Col Laurens agreed to the proposal. Col Hamilton observed, that unless the General was influenced by motives of personal enmity, he did not think the affair ought to be persued any further; but as General Lee seemed to persist in desiring it, he was too tender of his friend's honor to persist in opposing it. The combat was then going to be renewed; but Major Edwards again declaring his opinion, that the affair ought to end where it was, General Lee then expressed his confidence in the honor of the Gentlemen concerned as seconds, and said he should be willing to comply with whatever they should cooly and deliberately determine. Col. Laurens consented to the same....

[Stepping to one side, Hamilton and Edwards agreed that the duel should end. At the same time, Lee and Laurens discussed their differences more fully—and came to the same conclusion.]

On Col Hamilton's intimating the idea of personal enmity, as beforementioned, General Lee declared he had none, and had only met Col. Laurens to defend his own honor— that Mr. Laurens best knew whether there was any on his part. Col Laurens replied, that General Lee was acquainted with the motives, that had brought him there, which were that he had been informed from what he thought good authority, that General Lee had spoken of General Washington in the grossest and most opprobri-

Above: A South Carolina note for two shillings and six pence; below: a Continental note for four dollars

ous terms of personal abuse, which He Col Laurens thought himself bound to resent, as well on account of the relation he bore to General Washington as from motives of personal friendship, and respect for his character. General Lee acknowleged that he had given his opinion against General Washingtons military character to his particular friends and might perhaps do it again. He said every man had a right to give his sentiments freely of military characters, and that he did not think himself personally accountable to Col Laurens for what he had done in that respect. But said he never had spoken of General Washington in the terms mentioned, which he could not have done; as well because he had always esteemed General Washington as a man, as because such abuse would be incompatible with the character, he would ever wish to sustain as a Gentleman.

Upon the whole we think it a piece of justice to the two Gentlemen to declare, that after they met their conduct was strongly marked with all the politeness generosity coolness and firmness, that ought to characterise a transaction of this nature.

A few months later, Hamilton and his friend were separated when Laurens returned home to advocate a radical scheme for South Carolina's defense. Laurens hoped to raise battalions of slaves to supplement the militia; the black soldiers would be promised their freedom in return for their military service. When Laurens rode to Philadelphia to seek congressional endorsement of his plan, he carried the following letter of introduction from Hamilton to John Jay, then the president of Congress. Jay, a long-time opponent of slavery, could prove to be a valuable ally to Laurens.

[Middlebrook, New Jersey, March 14, 1779]
It appears to me, that an expedient of this kind, in the present state of Southern affairs, is the most rational, that can be adopted, and promises very important advantages. Indeed, I hardly see how a sufficient force can be collected in that quarter without it; and the enemy's operations there are growing infinitely serious and formidable. I have not the least doubt, that the negroes will make very excellent soldiers, with proper management.... It is a maxim with some great military judges, that with sensible officers soldiers can hardly be too stupid.... I mention this, because I frequently hear

it objected to the scheme of embodying negroes that they are too stupid to make soldiers. This is so far from appearing to me a valid objection that I think their want of cultivation (for their natural faculties are probably as good as ours) joined to that habit of subordination which they acquire from a life of servitude, will make them sooner became soldiers than our White inhabitants. Let officers be men of sense and sentiment, and the nearer the soldiers approach to machines perhaps the better.

I foresee that this project will have to combat much opposition from prejudice and self-interest. The contempt we have been taught to entertain for the blacks, makes us fancy many things that are founded neither in reason nor experience; and an unwillingness to part with property of so valuable a kind will furnish a thousand arguments to show the impracticability or pernicious tendency of a scheme which requires such a sacrifice. But it should be considered, that if we do not make use of them in this way, the enemy probably will; and that the best way to counteract the temptations they will hold out will be to offer them ourselves. An essential part of the plan is to give them their freedom with their muskets. This will secure their fidelity, animate their courage, and I believe will have a good influence upon those who remain, by opening a door to their emancipation. This circumstance, I confess, has no small weight in inducing me to wish the success of the project; for the dictates of humanity and true policy equally interest me in favour of this unfortunate class of men.

John Laurens

John Laurens's departure for South Carolina forced Hamilton to make a difficult and painful confession: he had allowed himself to grow fond of another human being. In a letter to Laurens, Hamilton did his best to explain his feelings and the reasons why he had tried, throughout most of his life, to avoid forming close friendships or "particular attachments."

[Middlebrook, New Jersey, April, 1779]
Cold in my professions, warm in my friendships, I wish, my Dear Laurens, it might be in my power, by action rather than words, to convince you that I love you. I shall only tell you that 'till you bade us Adieu, I hardly knew the value you had taught my heart to set upon you. Indeed, my friend, it was not well done. You know the

opinion I entertain of mankind, and how much it is my desire to preserve myself free from particular attachments, and to keep my happiness independent on the caprice of others. You should not have taken advantage of my sensibility to steal into my affections without my consent. But as you have done it and as we are generally indulgent to those we love, I shall not scruple to pardon the fraud you have committed, on condition that for my sake, if not for your own, you will always continue to merit the partiality, which you have so artfully instilled into me. . . .

[Having confided in Laurens this far, Hamilton let his thoughts turn to deeper attachments and, only half-jokingly, listed the qualifications he would wish to find in a wife.]

And Now my Dear as we are upon the subject of wife, I empower and command you to get me one in Carolina. Such a wife as I want will, I know, be difficult to be found, but if you succeed, it will be the stronger proof of your zeal and dexterity. Take her description—She must be young, handsome (I lay most stress upon a good shape) sensible (a little learning will do), well bred (but she must have an aversion to the word *ton*) chaste and tender (I am an enthusiast in my notions of fidelity and fondness) of some good nature, a great deal of generosity (she must neither love money nor scolding, for I dislike equally a termagent and an œconomist). In politics, I am indifferent what side she may be of; I think I have arguments that will easily convert her to mine. As to religion a moderate stock will satisfy me. She must believe in god and hate a saint. But as to fortune, the larger stock of that the better. You know my temper and circumstances and will therefore pay special attention to this article in the treaty. Though I run no risk of going to Purgatory for my avarice; yet as money is an essential ingredient to happiness in this world—as I have not much of my own and as I am very little calculated to get more either by my address or industry; it must needs be, that my wife, if I get one, bring at least a sufficiency to administer to her own extravagancies. NB You will be pleased to recollect in your negotiations that I have no invincible antipathy to the *maidenly beauties* & that I am willing to take the *trouble* of them upon myself.

If you should not readily meet with a lady that you think answers my description you can only advertise in the public papers and doubtless you will hear of many competitors for most of the qualifications required, who will be glad to become candidates for such a prize as I am. To excite their emulation, it will be necessary for you to give an account of the lover—his *size,* make, quality of mind and *body*, achievements, expectations, fortune, &c. In drawing my picture, you will no doubt be civil to your friend; mind you do justice to the length of my nose.

Hamilton diverted himself from the dull routine at camp that summer by composing a letter of introduction for Mrs. Judah Fitzgerald to present to Governor George Clinton of New York. Clinton, concerned for the outcome of an American expedition against the Iroquois in the western part of his state, was in sore need of the comic relief offered by Hamilton's letter.

[West Point, New York] Aug 24th. 79
The bearer of this is an *old woman* and of course the most troublesome animal in the world. She wants to go into New York. It was in vain we told her no inhabitant could be permitted by us to go within the enemy's lines without permission from the civil power. Old and decrepid as she is, she made the tour of the family and tried her blandishments upon each. I assured her Governor Clinton could have no possible motive for detaining her within his territories and would readily give his consent to her emigration. But nothing would satisfy her except a line from General Washington to the Governor. As she showed a disposition to remain with us 'till she carried her point, with true female perseverance— as we are rather straitened in our quarters, and not one of the Gentlemen of the family would agree to share his bed with her—And as you must at all events have the favour of a visit from her—I at last promised her a letter to you, the direct and sole end of which is to get rid of her. I dare say, your Excellency will think you make a very good bargain for the state, by getting rid of her also in the manner she wishes. She seems too to be in distress and have a claim upon our compassion.

Governor George Clinton

In the first week of September, Hamilton's good humor vanished. William Gordon, an eccentric Massachusetts clergyman, was spreading a story that Hamilton had declared that "it was high time for the people to rise, join General Washington, and turn Congress out of doors." Hamilton demanded that Gordon disclose the source of this tale, but the cleric tried to placate him with assurances that the words in question must have been spoken "unguardedly"; worse still, he refused to name the supposed witness to the incident until Hamilton promised not to challenge this mysterious informant to a duel. Furious, Hamilton sent this indignant reply to Gordon.

[West Point, New York, September 5, 1779] An opinion of my *inexperience* seems to have betrayed you into mistakes: Whatever you may imagine, Sir, I have read the *world* sufficiently to know that, though it may often be *convenient* to the propagator of a calumny to conceal the inventor, he will stand in need of no small address, to escape the suspicions & even the indignation of the honest & of the disinterested. Nor can I but persist in believing, that . . . the delicacy of your sentiments will be alarmed at the possibility of incurring this danger, & will prevent your exposing yourself to it, by refusing or delaying any longer, to comply with so reasonable a demand.

. . . The good sense of the present times has happily found out, that to prove your own innocence, or the malice of an accuser, the worst method, you can take, is to run him through the body, or shoot him through the head. And permit me to add, that while you felt an aversion to duelling, on the principles of religion, you ought, in charity, to have supposed others possessed of the same scruples, — of whose impiety you had no proofs. . . . The crime alleged to me is of such enormity, that, if I am guilty, it ought not to go unpunished; &, if I am innocent I should have an opportunity of indicating my innocence. The truth in either case should appear; & it is incumbent upon you, Sir, to afford the means, either by accusing me to my civil, or military superiors, or by disclosing the author of the information.

William Gordon

A few days later, renewing his correspondence with John Laurens, Hamilton reassessed America's position in view of Spain's recent declaration of war against England and predicted that the northern states no longer had much to fear from British arms.

The French Admiral Count D'Estaing

[West Point, New York, September 11, 1779]
Negotiation not conquest will then be [Britain's] object; the acquisition of two or three of the Southern states would be the counterballance to the loss of her Islands, give credit in Europe, facilitate honorable pacification or procure it. The plan of operations, I suppose in that case would be this—to evacuate Rhode Island, leave a garrison of eight thousand men for the defence of New York and its dependencies, detach five thousand to the West Indies to assist in garrisoning their remaining Islands, and then they will have five thousand to send to the Southward....

The plan here suggested, you will perhaps think with me is not the worst the enemy could adopt in their present circumstances. Its goodness is perhaps the strongest reason against its being undertaken; but they may blunder upon the right way for once, and we ought to be upon our guard.

In September, the Army's strategy was determined by naval considerations. The English fleet, under Admiral Arbuthnot, had reached New York, while the French Admiral Count D'Estaing had sailed to Georgia to aid in an assault on British-held Savannah. After conferring with the Chevalier de la Luzerne, France's minister to the United States, Washington made tentative plans for joint operations in the North. It was expected that D'Estaing would return soon from his Georgia expedition, and it was hoped that he would cooperate in some limited operation such as an attack upon New York City before sailing to the West Indies for the winter campaign. In order to communicate with the French admiral as quickly as possible, Hamilton and Brigadier General Louis Du Portail were sent to Philadelphia, where D'Estaing's fleet was to appear. After a few days, Hamilton and Du Portail pressed on to the New Jersey coast in hopes of sighting the elusive fleet, as they reported to Washington.

Great Egg Harbor Landing [New Jersey]
Octr. 26: 1779

We propose to remain till the arrival of the Count, till intelligence from him decides the inutility of a longer stay or 'till we receive your Excellency's orders of recall. We have now a better relation to the different points in which we are interested and have taken the necessary precautions to gain the earliest notice of whatever happens....

By recent information...we find that so late as the

fourth of this month the Count was yet to open his batteries against the enemy at Savannah. The time that will probably intervene between this and their final reduction . . . and his arrival on this coast may we fear exhaust the season too much to permit the cooperation to which our mission relates. We do not however despair; for if the Count has been fully successful to the Southward, and should shortly arrive which may be the case, the enterprise may possibly still go on.

Unwittingly, Washington had sent Hamilton on a wild goose chase. A week before Hamilton and Du Portail established their lonely outpost at Great Egg Harbor, D'Estaing had sailed for the West Indies, ignoring General Benjamin Lincoln's pleas that he continue the siege of Savannah; he thus had failed the American cause in Georgia as fully as he had a year before off Rhode Island. When Hamilton returned to headquarters at Morristown, there was yet another letter from William Gordon, in which the clergyman again refused to name his mysterious "informant." Thoroughly disgusted and having "no hope of bringing this affair to a more satisfactory conclusion," Hamilton put an end to the correspondence.

His fruitless search for D'Estaing and his message from William Gordon must have seemed to Hamilton an appropriate climax to a particularly frustrating period of his military career. He had seen no action since the Battle of Monmouth eighteen months earlier. His hopes for a part in a Franco-American expedition against New York were crushed. Furthermore, he had already begun to resent his work as Washington's aide. To a restless young man with dreams of glory, it must have seemed in December, 1779, that he had traded the hated "condition of a Clerk" in St. Croix for the same position in the Continental service. On the other hand, his experience on Washington's staff had given Hamilton a superb education in America's economic and political problems, and the warmth of that "family" enabled him to form close friendships. During the next two years that experience would serve him well in his efforts to find a more satisfying place in American life and the Continental Army.

Chapter 3

Triumphs in Love and War

To Americans of the second half of the twentieth century, Alexander Hamilton's obsession with military glory might seem rather puzzling, but for a young man who found himself, in 1780, with "no property here, no connexions," a reputation could be won most easily on the battlefield. For an ambitious man like Hamilton, military heroism had more than symbolic significance. Eventually, as a command in the field began to seem more and more elusive, Hamilton turned to other areas where "connexions" or "property" might be acquired. But at the beginning of 1780 he could see little future for himself in America. When he learned that his friend John Laurens had attempted to win a diplomatic assignment for him from Congress, Hamilton viewed the occasion as simply another proof of the futility of his life. In a letter to Laurens, Hamilton thanked his friend for his kindness, but made it clear that more than this would be needed to end his depression.

> [Morristown, New Jersey] Jany 8t. [1780]
> Believe me my Dr Laurens I am not insensible of the first mark of your affection in recommending me to your friends for a certain commission. However your partiality may have led you to overrate my qualifications that very partiality must endear you to me; and all the world will allow that your struggles and scruples upon the occasion deserve the envy of men of vertue....
>
> ...Not one of the four in nomination but would stand a better chance than myself; and yet my vanity tells me they do not all merit a preference. But I am a stranger in this country. I have no property here, no connexions. If I have talents and integrity, (as you say I have) these are justly deemed very spurious titles in these enlightened days, when unsupported by others more solid....

I have strongly sollicited leave to go to the Southward. It could not be refused; but arguments have been used to dissuade me from it, which however little weight they may have had in my judgment gave law to my feelings. I am chagrined and unhappy but I submit. In short Laurens I am disgusted with every thing in this world but yourself and *very* few more honest fellows and I have no other wish than as soon as possible to make a brilliant exit. 'Tis a weakness; but I feel I am not fit for this terrestreal Country.

Fortunately, the dull camp routine at Morristown during the winter of 1779–80 left Washington's family of young officers ample time for other diversions. A "dancing assembly" was formed, and the daughters of good patriots were only too delighted to participate. Among the ladies who visited headquarters was Elizabeth Schuyler, daughter of Major General Philip Schuyler. While the guest of her aunt and uncle in Morristown, "Betsey" caught Hamilton's eye and their romance progressed rapidly. In February, the young officer wrote to Elizabeth's sister Margarita, who had remained in Philadelphia where their father served in Congress. Although Hamilton had not met Margarita, he confessed to her that her older sister "by some odd contrivance" had "found out the secret of interesting me in every thing that concerns her."

[Morristown, New Jersey, February, 1780] I have already confessed the influence your sister has gained over me; yet notwithstanding this, I have some things of a very serious and heinous nature to lay to her charge. She is most unmercifully handsome and so perverse that she has none of those pretty affectations which are the prerogatives of beauty. Her good sense is destitute of that happy mixture of vanity and ostentation which would make it conspicuous to the whole tribe of fools and foplings as well as to men of understanding so that as the matter now stands it is very little known beyond the circle of these. She has good nature affability and vivacity unembellished with that charming frivolousness which is justly deemed one of the principal accomplishments of a *belle.* In short she is so strange a creature that she possesses all the beauties virtues and graces of her sex without any of those amiable defects, which from their general prevalence are esteemed by connoisseurs necessary shades in the character of a fine woman. The most determined adversaries of Hymen can

Philip Schuyler, by Trumbull

General Schuyler's headquarters at Morristown, where Hamilton and Elizabeth Schuyler first met

find in her no pretext for their hostility, and there are several of my friends, philosophers who railed at love as a weakness, men of the world who laughed at it as a phantasie, whom she has presumptuously and daringly compelled to acknowlege its power and surrender at discretion. I can the better assert the truth of this, as I am myself of the number. She has had the address to overset all the wise resolutions I had been framing for more than four years past, and from a rational sort of being and a professed contemner of Cupid has in a trice metamorphosed me into the veriest inamorato you perhaps ever saw.

In the second week of March, Hamilton's courtship was interrupted by the recurring problem of prisoners of war. On the ninth, Hamilton and two other officers set out for Perth Amboy, New Jersey, for negotiations with the British. As this tender letter to Elizabeth Schuyler clearly illustrates, Hamilton had declared his feelings before he left Morristown.

[Perth Amboy, New Jersey] Thursday Forenoon
[March 17, 1780]

My dearest girl

...Every moment of my stay here becomes more and more irksome; but I hope two or three days will put an end to it. Col Webb tells me you have sent for a carriage to go to Philadelphia. If you should set out before I return have the goodness to leave a line informing me how long you expect to be there. I beg too you will not suffer any considerations respecting me to prevent your going; for though it will be a tax upon my love to part with you so long, I wish you to see that city before you return.... Only let me entreat you to endeavour not to stay there longer than the amusements of the place interest you, in complaisance to friends; for you must always remember your best friend is where I am....

If I were not afraid of making you vain, I would tell you that Mrs. Carter, Peggy [Elizabeth Schuyler's sisters], and yourself are the dayly toasts of our table; and for this *honor* you are chiefly indebted to the British Gentlemen....

Our interview is attended with a great deal of sociability and good humour; but I begin notwithstanding to be tired of our British friends. They do their best to

Elizabeth Schuyler Hamilton

be agreeable and are particularly civil to me; but after all they are a compound of grimace and jargon; and out of a certain fashionable routine are as dull and empty as any Gentlemen need to be. One of their principal excellencies consists in swallowing a large quantity of wine every day, and in this I am so unfortunate that I shall make no sort of figure with them.

Returning to Morristown with his colleagues after two and a half weeks of fruitless negotiations with the British, Hamilton continued his courtship of Elizabeth Schuyler, who, he had now discovered, matched perfectly the requirements for a wife that he had sent to John Laurens in his half-joking letter of a year before. Not only would her father's influence as one of the wealthiest and most powerful men in New York more than compensate for Hamilton's own lack of connections; her good humor and even temper would make her an excellent wife for the sensitive, often moody, young officer. Philip Schuyler and his wife, journeying from Philadelphia to meet their daughter's suitor and consider his proposal, agreed to the match on April 8, and plans were made for a wedding in the late fall. But the prospect of a brilliant marriage did not distract Hamilton from other aspects of his "futurity." He still dreamed of military glory, and for a few days in June there seemed a chance of action. British forces under the Hessian General Knyphausen had landed near Elizabethtown, New Jersey, and Hamilton was sent forward to investigate the situation. From a vantage point near Springfield, New Jersey, he sent his report to Washington.

[Near Springfield, New Jersey, June 8, 1780] I have seen the enemy; those in view I calculate at about three thousand; there may be and probably enough are others out of sight. They have sent all their horse to the other side except about fifty or sixty. Their baggage it is agreed on all hands has also been sent across and their wounded. It is not ascertained that any of their infantry have passed to the other side....

Different conjectures may be made. The present movement may be calculated to draw us down and betray us into an action. They may have desisted from their intention of passing till night for fear of our falling upon their rear. I believe this is the case; for as they have but few boats it would certainly be a delicate manoeuvre to cross in our face. We are taking measures to watch their motions to night as closely as possible. An incessant but *very light* skirmishing.

The Jersey militia managed to halt the British raiders, and Hamilton returned to his duties as an aide. But, as he wrote to his friend John Laurens at the end of June, he was infuriated by the militia's poor showing and by the inability of the states to take joint action at this critical time.

[Ramapo, New Jersey, June 30, 1780]
My Dear Laurens, our countrymen have all the folly of the ass and all the passiveness of the sheep in their compositions. They are determined not to be free and they can neither be frightened, discouraged nor persuaded to change their resolution. If we are saved France and Spain must save us. I have the most pigmy-feelings at the idea, and I almost wish to hide my disgrace in universal ruin. Don't think I rave; for the conduct of the states is enough most pitiful that can be imagined. Would you believe it—a German baron at the head of five thousand men, in the month of June insulted and defied the main American army with the Commander in Chief at their head with impunity, and made them tremble for the security of their magazines forty miles in the country.

The Schuyler home near Albany (above) and Schuyler's mills (below) were destroyed by the British in 1777 and rebuilt after the war.

The military situation was not as bleak as Hamilton believed it to be. Lafayette had recently returned from France with news of substantial aid—an expeditionary force under the capable Comte de Rochambeau. Hamilton's mood may have been affected by Elizabeth's departure for Albany. Lonely and miserable, he wrote to her early in July.

[Preakness, New Jersey, July 2–4, 1780]
I love you more and more every hour. The sweet softness and delicacy of your mind and manners, the elevation of your sentiments, the real goodness of your heart, its tenderness to me, the beauties of your face and person, your unpretending good sense and that innocent simplicity and frankness which pervade your actions; all these appear to me with increasing amiableness and place you in my estimation above all the rest of your sex.

I entreat you my Charmer, not to neglect the charges I gave you particularly that of taking care of your self, and that of employing all your leisure in reading. Nature has been very kind to you; do not neglect to cultivate her gifts and to enable yourself to make the distinguished figure in all respects to which you are intitled to aspire. You excel most of your sex in all the amiable qualities; endeavour to excel them equally in the splendid ones.

You can do it if you please and I shall take pride in it. It will be a fund too, to diversify our enjoyments and amusements and fill all our moments to advantage....

Yrs. my Angel with inviolable Affection

ALEX HAMILTON

While watching impatiently with the rest of Washington's staff for the appearance of Rochambeau's fleet, Hamilton complained to Betsey Schuyler that his affection for her prevented him from enjoying anything else.

Col. Dey's house Bergen County [New Jersey]
July 6th. [1780]

Here we are my love in a house of great hospitality — in a country of plenty — a buxom girl under the same roof — pleasing expectations of a successful campaign — and every thing to make a soldier happy, who is not in love and absent from his mistress. As this is my case I cannot be happy; but it is a maxim of my life to enjoy the present good with the highest relish & to soften the present evil by a hope of future good. I alleviate the pain of absence by looking forward to that delightful period which gives us to each other forever; and my imagination serves up such a feast of pleasure as almost makes me forget the deprivation I now experience. But alas my Dear girl this does not always do. The illusion will not always soothe; my heart every now and then cries: You are separated from the lovely partner of your life; four long months must elapse before this separation ends; your sweet girl with nothing to engage or divert her attention is perhaps suffering the keenest anxiety for the situation of her lover not only absent from her but exposed to a thousand imaginary dangers.

But my dearest quiet your apprehensions (for I know your tender fond mind is of too apprehensive a cast) and let your thoughts run only upon those delights which our reunion will afford.

Adieu my angel, be happy and love me as well as I love you

A HAMILTON

Comte de Rochambeau, by Peale

Rochambeau reached Newport four days later and Lafayette was sent north to "fix our plan of operations" with the French commander. Both Lafayette and Hamilton were hoping that allied strategy would involve an attack on New York City, where both could win military fame, and in mid-July, Hamilton wrote of their scheme to François de Barbé-Marbois, the young secretary to the French diplomatic mission in Philadelphia.

[Preakness, New Jersey, July 20, 1780] New York in all probability will be our object; if we can have a naval superiority, I shall not doubt our success; if we have not the event will be very precarious; and in success the advantages infinitely less. The enemy will save a great part of their army; stores & their shipping of course will be safe, and the whole may fall upon some other part where we may be vulnerable.

I shall take occasion to assure you that it appears clear to a demonstration that with a superiority by land and sea you can infallibly possess the port of New York, and by seige or blockade, reduce the whole fleet and army. What will be done or can be done to secure an object of such magnitude, I cannot judge; only of this I am confident that your court will do every thing possible. The proofs she has already given would make it ingratitude to doubt her future intentions.

François de Barbé-Marbois

Hope for an early campaign against New York faded when a British fleet under Admiral Thomas Graves threatened French forces at Newport. Washington marched north to divert British attention and naval power from Rhode Island, and by August not even Hamilton could pretend that a New York campaign was likely. His dreams of an early military expedition died hard, and the unpleasant turn of events even affected his attitude toward his marriage. Writing to Elizabeth Schuyler late in August, Hamilton began in a lighthearted fashion but soon adopted a more serious tone.

[Teaneck, New Jersey, August, 1780] Though I am not sanguine in expecting it, I am not without hopes this Winter will produce a peace and then you must submit to the mortification of enjoying more domestic happiness and less fame. This I know you will not like, but we cannot always have things as we wish.

The affairs of England are in so bad a plight that if no fortunate events attend her this campaign, it would seem impossible for her to proceed in the war. But she is an obstinate old dame, and seems determined to ruin her whole family, rather than to let Miss America go on

Rochambeau's forces step ashore at Newport, Rhode Island, July, 1780.

flirting it with her new lovers, with whom, as giddy young girls often do, she eloped in contempt of her mothers authority. I know you will be ready to justify her conduct and tell me the ill treatment she received was enough to make any girl of spirit act in the same manner. But I will one day cure you of these refractory notions about the right of resistance, (of which I foresee you will be apt to make a very dangerous application), and teach you the great advantage and absolute necessity of implicit obedience.

But now we are talking of times to come, tell me my pretty damsel have you made up your mind upon the subject of housekeeping? Do you soberly relish the pleasure of being a poor mans wife? Have you learned to think a home spun preferable to a brocade and the rumbling of a waggon wheel to the musical rattling of a coach and six?...If you cannot my Dear we are playing a comedy of all in the wrong, and you should correct the mistake before we begin to act the tragedy of the unhappy couple.

Hamilton had meantime found an engrossing pastime to distract him from his loneliness. Long critical of American government, he now began formulating remedies for the nation's ills. In a letter to James Duane, New York's powerful congressman, he outlined his developing political theories and discussed the need for a strong central government that could provide "method and energy" in administering America's affairs. As a spokesman for administrative reform in Congress, Duane could be counted on to listen carefully to Hamilton's "ideas on the defects of our present system, and the changes necessary to save us from ruin."

[Liberty Pole, New Jersey, September 3, 1780] The fundamental defect is a want of power in Congress. It is hardly worth while to show in what this consists, as it seems to be universally acknowleged, or to point out how it has happened, as the only question is how to remedy it. It may however be said that it has originated from three causes—an excess of the spirit of liberty which has made the particular states show a jealousy of all power not in their own hands; and this jealousy has led them to exercise a right of judging in the last resort of the measures recommended by Congress, and of acting according to their own opinions of their propriety or necessity, a diffidence in Congress of their own powers, by which they have been timid and indecisive in their resolutions, constantly making concessions to the states, till they have scarcely left themselves the shadow of power; a want of sufficient means at their disposal to answer the public exigencies and of vigor to draw forth those means; which have occasioned them to depend on the states individually to fulfill their engagements with the army, and the consequence of which has been to ruin their influence and credit with the army, to establish its dependence on each state separately rather than *on them*, that is rather than on the whole collectively....

Another defect in our system is want of method and energy in the administration. This has partly resulted from the other defect, but in a great degree from prejudice and the want of a proper executive. Congress have kept the power too much into their own hands and have meddled too much with details of every sort. Congress is properly a deliberative corps and it forgets itself when it attempts to play the executive. It is impossible such a body, numerous as it is, constantly fluctuating, can ever act with sufficient decision, or with system. Two thirds of the members, one half the time, cannot know what has gone before them or what connection the subject in hand has to what has been transacted on former occasions. The members, who have been more permanent, will only give information, that promotes the side they espouse, in the present case, and will as often mislead as enlighten....

The first step must be to give Congress powers competent to the public exigencies. This may happen in two ways, one by resuming and exercising the discretionary powers I suppose to have been originally vested in them for the safety of the states...the other by calling immediately a convention of all the states with full authority to conclude finally upon a general confederation, stating to them beforehand explicitly the evils arising from a want of power in Congress, and the impossibility of supporting the contest on its present footing, that the delegates may come possessed of proper sentiments as well as proper authority to give to the meeting....

...The Convention should assemble the 1st of November next, the sooner, the better; our disorders are too violent to admit of a common or lingering remedy.... A convention may agree upon a confederation; the states individually hardly ever will. We must have one at all

In this British cartoon of 1779, the horse "America" is shown throwing his master, George III.

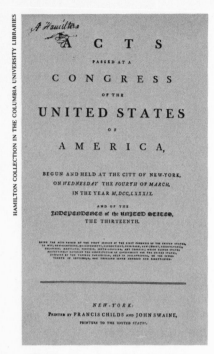

Hamilton's copy of the 1780 "Acts of Congress" bears his signature.

The Continental Congress, 1780, as shown in an English engraving

events, and a vigorous one if we mean to succeed in the contest and be happy hereafter.... Congress ought to confess ... plainly and unanimously the impracticability of supporting our affairs on the present footing and without a solid coercive union....

The second step I would recommend is that Congress should instantly appoint the following great officers of state—A secretary for foreign affairs—a President of war—A President of Marine—a Financier—A President of trade....

Congress should choose for these offices, men of the first abilities, property and character in the continent—and such as have had the best opportunities of being acquainted with the several branches....

These offices should have nearly the same powers and functions as those in France analogous to them, and each should be chief in his department, with subordinate boards composed of assistant clerks &c. to execute his orders....

[Next, Congress must reform the American Army. Under Hamilton's plan, terms of enlistment were to be standardized, and officers were to be rewarded with a pension of "half pay"—a yearly payment equal to half their annual salaries in the Army.]

The advantages of securing the attachment of the army to Congress, and binding them to the service by substantial ties are immense. We should then have discipline, an army in reality, as well as in name. Congress would then have a solid basis of authority and consequence, for to me it is an axiom that in our constitution an army is essential to the American union.

The providing of supplies is the pivot of every thing else.... There are four ways all which must be united—a foreign loan, heavy pecuniary taxes, a tax in kind, a bank founded on public and private credit.

As to a foreign loan I dare say, Congress are doing every thing in their power to obtain it. The most effectual way will be to tell France that without it, we must make terms with great Britain....

Concerning the necessity of heavy pecuniary taxes I need say nothing, as it is a point in which everybody is agreed....

As to a tax in kind, the necessity of it results from this principle—that the money in circulation is not a sufficient representative of the productions of the country. . . .

How far it may be practicable to erect a bank on the joint credit of the public and of individuals can only be certainly determined by the experiment; but it is of so much importance that the experiment ought to be fully tried. . . .

If a Convention is called the minds of all the states and the people ought to be prepared to receive its determinations by sensible and popular writings, which should conform to the views of Congress. There are epochs in human affairs, when *novelty* even is useful. If a general opinion prevails that the old way is bad, whether true or false, and this obstructs or relaxes the operation of the public service, a change is necessary if it be but for the sake of change. This is exactly the case now. 'Tis an universal sentiment that our present system is a bad one, and that things do not go right on this account. The measure of a Convention would revive the hopes of the people and give a new direction to their passions, which may be improved in carrying points of substantial utility. . . .

And, in future, My Dear Sir, two things let me recommend, as fundamental rules for the conduct of Congress—to attach the army to them by every motive, to maintain an air of authority (not domineering) in all their measures with the states. The manner in which a thing is done has more influence than is commonly imagined. Men are governed by opinion; this opinion is as much influenced by appearances as by realities; if a Government appears to be confident of its own powers, it is the surest way to inspire the same confidence in others; if it is diffident, it may be certain, there will be a still greater diffidence in others, and that its authority will not only be distrusted, controverted, but contemned.

James Duane helped draft the Articles of Confederation and later became the mayor of New York.

Before he could dispatch his letter to Duane, Hamilton heard of Horatio Gates's defeat at Camden, South Carolina, on August 16—a battle that has been described as "the most disastrous defeat ever inflicted on an American army." Gates compounded his disgrace by retreating at record speed, putting almost two hundred miles between himself and the remnants of the Southern Army in three and a half days. Writing again to Duane,

Hamilton did not miss this chance to bolster his arguments for Army reform and to attack his old enemy, Gates.

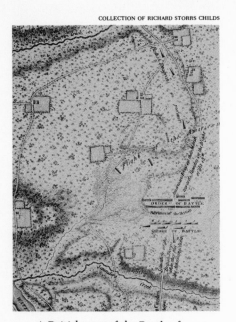

COLLECTION OF RICHARD STORRS CHILDS

A British map of the Battle of Camden, South Carolina—a disaster for America's Southern Army

[Bergen County, New Jersey] Sept 6. 1780
I have heard since of Gates defeat, a very good comment on the necessity of changing our system.... What think you of the conduct of this great man? I am his enemy personally, for unjust and unprovoked attacks upon my character, therefore what I say of him ought to be received as from an enemy.... But did ever any one hear of such a disposition or such a flight? His best troops placed on the side strongest by nature, his worst, on that weakest by nature, and his attack made with these. 'Tis impossible to give a more complete picture of military absurdity. It is equally against the maxims of war, and common sense....

But was there ever an instance of a General running away as Gates has done from his whole army? and was there ever so precipitous a flight? One hundred and eighty miles in three days and a half. It does admirable credit to the activity of a man at his time of life. But it disgraces the General and the Soldiers.

Meanwhile, Hamilton's fight for reform was winning him enemies on all sides in Congress and in the Army. As he explained in a letter to John Laurens, his position was becoming increasingly difficult.

[New Bridge, New Jersey, September 12, 1780]
You told me, my remedies were good, but you were afraid would not go down at this time. I tell you necessity must force them down; and that if they are not speedily taken the patient will die. She is in a gallopping consumption, and her case will soon become desperate. Indeed, my Dear friend, to drop allegory, you can hardly conceive in how dreadful a situation we are. The army, in the course of the present month, has received only four or five days rations of meal, and we really know not of any adequate relief in future.... The officers are out of humour.... 'Tis in vain you attempt to appease; you are almost detested as an accomplice with the administration. I am losing character my friend, because I am not over complaisant to the spirit of clamour, so that I am in a fair way to be out with every body. With one set, I am considered as a friend to military pretensions however exorbitant, with another as a man, who secured by my

situation from sharing the distress of the army, am inclined to treat it lightly. The truth is I am an unlucky, honest man, that speak my sentiments to all and with emphasis. I say this to you because you know it and will not charge me with vanity. I hate Congress—I hate the army—I hate the world—I hate myself. The whole is a mass of fools and knaves; I could almost except you and [Richard Kidder] Meade.

In the last week of September, Hamilton accompanied Washington to Hartford, Connecticut, for conferences with the French. On their return journey, they witnessed an incident that temporarily overshadowed any disappointments over French aid or congressional inefficiency. For sixteen months, Benedict Arnold, the American commander at West Point, had been secretly negotiating with the British, and by the end of August, 1780, he had agreed to surrender the plans of fortifications at West Point. Sir Henry Clinton's aide, John André, was sent north to meet Arnold's agent, Joshua Hett Smith, but at 9 A.M. on September 25, Arnold learned that Smith and André had been captured. Washington and his party were to arrive at West Point later in the day, and Arnold lost no time in departing for safety to New York City. By the time Washington and Hamilton reached West Point, Arnold had vanished, and, as Hamilton reported to Elizabeth Schuyler, Washington's aides had to deal with the traitor's hysterical wife.

[Robinson's House, Highlands, New York]
Sepr 25 [1780]

The fortifications at West Point, as seen at the close of the war

In the midst of my letter, I was interrupted by a scene that shocked me more than any thing I have met with—the discovery of a treason of the deepest dye. The object was to sacrifice West Point. General Arnold had sold himself to André for this purpose. The latter came but in disguise and in returning to New York was detected. Arnold hearing of it immediately fled to the enemy. I went in persuit of him but was much too late, and I could hardly regret the disappointment, when on my return, I saw an amiable woman frantic with distress for the loss of a husband she tenderly loved—a traitor to his country and to his fame, a disgrace to his connections. It was the most affecting scene I ever was witness to. She for a considerable time intirely lost her senses. The General went up to see her and she upbraided him with being in a plot to murder her child; one moment she raved; another she melted into tears; sometimes she

89

Margaret Shippen Arnold, as
sketched by Major André in 1778

pressed her infant to her bosom and lamented its fate occasioned by the imprudence of its father in a manner that would have pierced insensibility itself. . . . We have every reason to believe she was intirely unacquainted with the plan, and that her first knowlege of it was when Arnold went to tell her he must banish himself from his Country and from her forever. She instantly fell into a convulsion and he left her in that situation.

This morning she is more composed. I paid her a visit and endeavoured to sooth her by every method in my power, though you may imagine she is not easily to be consoled. Added to her other distresses, She is very apprehensive the resentment of her country will fall upon her . . . for the guilt of her husband. . . . She received us in bed, with every circumstance that could interest our sympathy. Her sufferings were so eloquent that I wished myself her brother, to have a right to become her defender. As it is, I have entreated her to enable me to give her proofs of my friendship.

Could I forgive Arnold for sacrificing his honor reputation and duty I could not forgive him for acting a part that must have forfieted the esteem of so fine a woman. At present she almost forgets his crime in his misfortune, and her horror at the guilt of the traitor is lost in her love of the man. But a virtuous mind cannot long esteem a base one, and time will make her despise, if it cannot make her hate.

Margaret Shippen Arnold, who was well aware of her husband's plans, did not deserve Hamilton's chivalrous concern, although she certainly should have won his applause for her acting ability. Another party in the scheme, Major John André, was a more sympathetic figure. The young British officer charmed his captors, and when André was judged a spy and sentenced to hang, Hamilton did his best to give the Englishman what help he could. On the day of André's death, Hamilton explained his conduct to Elizabeth Schuyler.

[Tappan, New York, October 2, 1780]
To justify myself to your sentiments, I must inform you that I urged a compliance with Andre's request to be shot and I do not think it would have had an ill effect; but some people are only sensible to motives of policy, and sometimes from a narrow disposition mistake it. When André's tale comes to be told, and present resentment is

over, the refusing him the privilege of choosing the manner of death will be branded with too much obduracy.

It was proposed to me to suggest to him the idea of an exchange for Arnold; but I knew I should have forfieted his esteem by doing it, and therefore declined it. As a man of honor he could not but reject it and I would not for the world have proposed to him a thing, which must have placed me in the unamiable light of supposing him capable of a meanness, or of not feeling myself the impropriety of the measure. I confess to you I had the weakness to value the esteem of a *dying* man; because I reverenced his merit.

Nine days after André's execution (by hanging), Hamilton sent a lengthy account of the English officer's story to John Laurens. "Never," he told Laurens, "did any man suffer death with more justice, or deserve it less."

[Preakness, New Jersey, October 11, 1780] There was something singularly interesting in the character and fortunes of André. To an excellent understanding well improved by education and travel, he united a peculiar elegance of mind and manners, and the advantage of a pleasing person. . . . By his merit he had acquired the unlimited confidence of his general and was making a rapid progress in military rank and reputation. But in the height of his career, flushed with new hope from the execution of a project the most beneficial to his party . . . he was at once precipitated from the summit . . . and saw all the expectations of his ambition blasted and himself ruined. . . .

. . . In going to the place of execution, he bowed familiarly as he went along to all those with whom he had been acquainted in his confinement. A smile of complacency expressed the serene fortitude of his mind. Arrived at the fatal spot, he asked with some emotion, *must* I then die in this manner? He was told it had been unavoidable. "I am reconciled to my fate (said he) but not to the mode." Soon however recollecting himself, he added, "it will be but a momentary pang," and springing upon the cart performed the last offices to himself with a composure that excited the admiration and melted the hearts of the beholders. Upon being told the final moment was at hand, and asked if he had any thing to say, he answered:

André made these sketches the day before his execution: a self-portrait and a view of his crossing of the Hudson for his meeting with Arnold.

"nothing, but to request you will witness to the world, that I die like a brave man."

By the end of October, Hamilton was thinking of little besides his plans for marriage. He confessed to Betsey that she occupied his sleeping as well as his waking hours, and as proof he wrote his "Dear girl" an account of a dream he had had.

> [Preakness, New Jersey, October 27, 1780]
> I had a charming dream two or three night ago. I thought I had just arrived at Albany and found you asleep on a green near the house, and beside you in an inclined posture stood a Gentleman whom I did not know. He had one of your hands in his, and seemed fixed in silent admiration. As you may imagine, I reproached him with his presumption and asserted my claim. He insisited on a prior right; and the dispute grew heated. This I fancied awoke you, when yielding to a sudden impulse of joy, you flew into my arms and decided the contention with a kiss. I was so delighted that I immediately waked, and lay the rest of the night exulting in my good fortune. Tell me pray you who is this rival of mine. Dreams you know are the messengers of Jove.

Hamilton's wedding plans were delayed when two of Washington's other aides were called home to Virginia. While he waited for these officers to return and relieve him, Hamilton used his time to work out another plan for a New York expedition with Lafayette. Although Washington had refused to consider his earlier requests for a command in the field, Hamilton wrote again to his commander in hopes of persuading him that he could serve in this projected campaign.

> [Passaic Falls, New Jersey, November 22, 1780]
> Sometime last fall when I spoke to your Excellency about going to the Southward, I explained to you candidly my feelings with respect to military reputation, and how much it was my object to act a conspicuous part in some enterprise that might perhaps raise my character as a soldier above mediocrity. You were so good as to say you would be glad to furnish me with an occasion. When the expedition to Staten Island was on foot a favourable one seemed to offer.... I made an application for it through the Marquis, who informed me of your refusal on two principles—one that giving me a

whole batalion might be a subject of dissatisfaction, the other that if an accident should happen to me, in the present state of your family, you would be embarrassed for the necessary assistance.

The project you now have in contemplation affords another opportunity. I have a variety of reasons that press me to desire ardently to have it in my power to improve it. . . .

I take this method of making the request to avoid the embarrassment of a personal explanation; I shall only add that however much I have the matter at heart, I wish your Excellency intirely to consult your own inclination; and not from a disposition to oblige me, to do any thing, that may be disagreeable to you. It will, nevertheless, make me singularly happy if your wishes correspond with mine.

Hamilton's request for a military command was again turned down. But if there was to be no military glory for him in 1780, the young officer could console himself with the prospect of a happy marriage. At the end of November, he rode to Albany, where he and Elizabeth Schuyler were married on December 14. Married life agreed with him perfectly, as he confessed to his sister-in-law Margarita Schuyler soon after his return to headquarters.

A reception given by General and Mrs. Washington (right), to honor Hamilton and his bride, who are seen at left, beneath the chandelier

[New Windsor, New York, January 21, 1781] Because your sister has the talent of growing more amiable every day, or because I am a fanatic in love, or both—or if you prefer another interpretation, because I have address enough to be a good dissembler, she fancies herself the happiest woman in the world, and would need persuade all her friends to embark with her in the matrimonial voyage. But I pray you do not let her advice have so much influence as to make you matrimony-mad. 'Tis a very good thing when their stars unite two people who are fit for each other, who have souls capable of relishing the sweets of friendship, and sensibilities. . . . But its a dog of life when two dissonant tempers meet, and 'tis ten to one but this is the case. When therefore I join her in advising you to marry, I add be cautious in the choice. Get a man of sense, not ugly enough to be pointed at—with some good-nature—a few grains of feeling—a little taste—a little imagination—and above all a good deal of decision to keep you in order; for that I foresee will be no easy task. If you can find one with all these qualities, willing to marry you, marry him as soon as you please.

I must tell you in confidence that I think I have been very fortunate.

By early 1781, prospects for military and civilian reform had improved considerably. Mutiny among Continental troops in New Jersey and Pennsylvania had persuaded Congress to consider the plan for executive "departments" that James Duane had prepared six months before; and after three years, Maryland at last seemed ready to ratify the Articles of Confederation. Still, as Hamilton confided to Barbé-Marbois, it was too early to rejoice.

[New Windsor, New York, February 7, 1781] The first step to reformation as well in an administration as in an individual is to be sensible of our faults. This begins to be our case; and there are several symptoms that please me at this juncture. But we are so accustomed to doing right by halves, and spoiling a good intention in the execution, that I always wait to see the end of our public arrangements before I venture to expect good or ill from them. The plan of executive ministers is undoubtedly a good one, and by some men has been fruitlessly insisted upon for three or four years back; but whether it will work a present good or evil must depend on the choice of the persons. This is a bad omen. I am not at all informed of the persons in nomination.

The accession of Maryland to the confederacy will be a happy event if it does not make people believe that the Confederacy gives Congress power enough and prevent their acquiring more; if it has this effect it will be an evil, for it is unequal to the exigencies of the war or to the preservation of the union hereafter.

Nine days later, Hamilton's place in the Continental military establishment was threatened. His frustrations as an aide, his failure to gain a command, had finally taken their toll on the headstrong young officer. In mid-February, Hamilton wrote to his father-in-law of an "unexpected change" in his situation.

Head Quarters New Windsor [New York] Feby 18, 81 I am no longer a member of the General's family. This information will surprise you and the manner of the change will surprise you more. Two day ago The General

Washington, Tilghman, and Lafayette at Yorktown, by C. W. Peale, 1784

and I passed each other on the stairs. He told me he wanted to speak to me. I answered that I would wait upon him immediately. I went below and delivered Mr. Tilghman [Lieutenant Colonel Tench Tilghman] a letter to be sent to The Commissary containing an order of a pressing and interesting nature. Returning to The General I was stopped in the way by the Marquis De la Fayette and we conversed together about a minute on a matter of business. He can testify how impatient I was to get back, and that I left him in a manner which but for our intimacy would have been more than abrupt. Instead of finding the General as usual in his room, I met him at the head of the stairs, where accosting me in a very angry tone, "Col Hamilton (said he), you have kept me waiting at the head of the stairs these ten minutes. I must tell you Sir you treat me with disrespect." I replied without petulancy, but with decision "I am not conscious of it Sir, but since you have thought it necessary to tell me so we part" "Very well Sir (said he) if it be your choice" or something to this effect and we separated.

I sincerely believe my absence which gave so much umbrage did not last two minutes.

In less than an hour after, Tilghman came to me in the Generals name assuring me of his great confidence in my abilities, integrity usefulness &c and of his desire in a candid conversation to heal a difference which could not have happened but in a moment of passion. I requested Mr. Tilghman to tell him, 1. that I had taken my resolution in a manner not to be revoked: 2. that as a conversation could serve no other purpose than to produce explanations mutually disagreeable, though I certainly would not refuse an interview if he desired it yet I should be happy he would permit me to decline it—3. that though determined to leave the family the same principles which had kept me so long in it would continue to direct my conduct towards him when out of it. 4. that however I did not wish to distress him or the public business, by quitting him before he could derive other assistance by the return of some of the Gentlemen who were absent: 5. And that in the mean time it depended on him to let our behaviour to each other be the same as if nothing had happened.

He consented to decline the conversation and thanked me for my offer of continuing my aid, in the manner I had mentioned.

Thus we stand. . . .

I always disliked the office of an Aide de Camp as having in it a kind of personal dependance. I refused to serve in this capacity with two Major General's at an early period of the war. Infected however with the enthusiasm of the times, an idea of the Generals character which experience soon taught me to be unfounded overcame my scruples and induced me to *accept his invitation* to enter into his family. I believe you know the place I held in The Generals confidence and councils of which will make it the more extraordinary to you to learn that for three years past I have felt no friendship for him and have professed none. The truth is our own dispositions are the opposites of each other & the pride of my temper would not suffer me to profess what I did not feel. Indeed when advances of this kind have been made to me on his part they were received in a manner that showed at least I had no inclination to court them, and that I wished to stand rather upon a footing of military confidence than of private attachment. You are too good a judge of human nature not to be sensible how this conduct in me must have operated on a man to whom all the world is offering incense. With this key you will easily unlock the present mystery. At the end of the war I may say many things to you concerning which I shall impose upon myself 'till then an inviolable silence.

The General is a very honest man. His competitors have slender abilities and less integrity. His popularity has often been essential to the safety of America, and is still of great importance to it. These considerations have influenced my past conduct respecting him, and will influence my future. I think it is necessary he should be supported.

His estimation in your mind, whatever may be its amounts, I am persuaded has been formed on principles which a circumstance like this cannot materially affect; but if I thought it could diminish your friendship for him, I should almost forego the motives that urge me to justify myself to you. I wish what I have said to make no other impression than to satisfy you I have not been in the wrong. It is also said in confidence, for as a public knowledge of the breach would in many ways have an ill effect. it will probably be the policy of both sides to conceal it and cover the separation with some plausible pretext. I am importuned by such friends as are privy to the affair, to listen to a reconciliation: but my resolution is unalterable.

With his departure from headquarters not far off, Hamilton began sounding out friends on other opportunities in the Continental service. He cautiously wrote on the subject to Nathanael Greene, Gates's successor as commander of the Southern Army.

> Hd. Qrs. New Windsor [New York] April 19. 81
> [Robert Hanson] Harrison has left the General to be a Chief Justice of Maryland. I am about leaving him to be anything that fortune may cast up. I mean in the military line. This, my dear General, is not an affair of calculation but of feeling. You may divine the rest, and I am sure you will keep your divinations to yourself.
>
> The enemy have gotten so much in the way of intercepting our mails that I am afraid of seeing whatever I write spring up the Week after in Rivingtons Gazette. This obliges me to be cautious. Adieu, My Dear General. Let me beg you will believe that whatever change there may be in my situation there never will be any in my respect, esteem, and affection for you.
>
> A HAMILTON
>
> PS. Let me know if I could find any thing worth my while to do in the Southern army. You know I shall hate to be nominally a soldier.

A view of Albany, 1789

Late in April, Hamilton made one more appeal to Washington for a command in the field. When his request was refused, the disheartened young officer, together with his wife, Elizabeth, left for an extended visit with the Schuyler family in Albany. Historians can only guess at Hamilton's reasons for suddenly interrupting this vacation at the beginning of July to hurry to Washington's new camp at Dobbs Ferry, New York. Perhaps he was shrewd enough to see that this would be the year in which the French alliance would secure Britain's defeat, and that the fall campaign would be his last opportunity to serve. Perhaps he simply became bored with the quiet town of Albany. In any case, shortly after his arrival at Dobbs Ferry on July 8, Hamilton was writing triumphantly to his wife.

> [Camp near Dobbs Ferry, New York, July 10, 1781]
> Finding when I came here that nothing was said on the

subject of a command, I wrote the General a letter and enclosed him my commission. This morning Tilghman came to me in his name, pressed me to retain my commission, with an assurance that he would endeavor by all means to give me a command nearly such as I could have desired in the present circumstances of the army. Though I know my Betsy would be happy to hear I had rejected this proposal, it is a pleasure my reputation would not permit me to afford her. I consented to retain my commission and accept my command.

I hope my beloved Betsy will dismiss all apprehensions for my safety; unhappily for public affairs, there seems to be little prospect of activity, and if there should be Heaven will certainly be propitious to any attachment so tender, so genuine as ours....

My good, my tender, my fond, my excellent Betsy, Adieu. You know not how much it must ever cost me to pronounce this word. God bless and preserve you.

Troops at Dobbs Ferry saw little action that month as Washington and Rochambeau debated whether to attack Sir Henry Clinton's forces in New York City or to strike at the army of Charles, Lord Cornwallis, in Virginia. While the American and French commanders weighed the reports of their scouts, Hamilton wrote to his young wife.

[Dobbs Ferry, New York, July 13, 1781]
I remonstrate with my heart on the impropriety of suffering itself to be engrossed by an individual of the human race when so many millions ought to participate in its affections and in its cares. But it constantly presents you under such amiable forms as seem too well to justify its meditated desertion of the cause of country humanity, and of glory I would say, if there were not something in the sound insipid and ridiculous....

Indeed Betsey, I am intirely changed—changed for the worse I confess—lost to all the public and splendid passions and absorbed in you. Amiable woman! nature has given you a right to be esteemed to be cherished, to be beloved; but she has given you no right to monopolize a man, whom, to you I may say, she has endowed with qualities to be extensively useful to society.... Assist me in this; reproach me for an unmanly surrender...to love and teach me that your esteem will be the price of my acting well my part as a member of society.

On August 14, Washington learned that the French fleet of the Comte de Grasse had sailed for Chesapeake Bay. Plans for an attack on New York were discarded and the Yorktown campaign was born. On the evening of August 20, the French army and half of the Continental forces at Dobbs Ferry began their historic march south to Virginia. In a letter written at Haverstraw, New York, Hamilton gently broke the news to his wife.

Haverstraw [New York] Aug 22d. 81

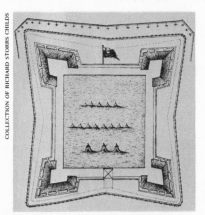

Plan of a typical British redoubt of the Revolutionary period

A part of the army My Dear girl is going to Virginia, and I must of necessity be separated at a much greater distance from my beloved wife....I am unhappy beyond expression, I am unhappy because I am to be so remote from you, because I am to hear from you less frequently than I have been accustomed to do....I am wretched at the idea of flying so far from you without a single hour's interview to tell you all my pains and all my love. But I cannot ask permission to visit you. It might be thought improper to leave my corps at such a time and upon such an occasion. I cannot persuade myself to ask a favour at Head Quarters. I must go without seeing you. I must go without embracing you. Alas I must go.

Expecting relief from the British navy, Cornwallis confidently withdrew his forces to the towns of Yorktown and Gloucester Point, on opposite banks of the York River. But the French navy, which had disappointed Americans so often in the past, now proved its worth by blocking the British fleet. As Hamilton waited on the Virginia peninsula for the siege of Yorktown to begin, he received word from Elizabeth that she was pregnant and that their first child would be born in January. Hamilton immediately wrote to his "darling Wife," his "beloved Angel."

[Camp before Yorktown, Virginia,
October 12, 1781]

You shall engage shortly to present me with *a boy.* You will ask me if a girl will not answer the purpose. By no means. I fear, with all the mothers charms, she may inherit the caprices of her father and then she will enslave, tantalize and plague one half the sex, out of pure regard to which I protest against a daughter....

In an instant my feelings are changed. My heart disposed to gayety is at once melted into tenderness. The idea of a smiling infant in my Betseys arms calls up all the father in it. In imagination I embrace the mother and embrace the child a thousand times. I can scarce refrain from shedding tears of joy. But I must not indulge these sensations; they are unfit for the boisterous scenes of war and whenever they intrude themselves make me but half a soldier.

Two days later, Hamilton found the military glory he had been seeking for so long. To strengthen their position, the Allies had to capture the British "redoubts" numbered 9 and 10 near the York River. These redoubts were temporary posts surrounded by earthworks, ditches, and other barriers. Lafayette was given command of the assault on number 10, and after considerable wrangling over the rights of rank, his friend Hamilton was given the honor of leading the four hundred men who actually attacked the post. At nightfall on October 14, six cannon fired their signal, and Hamilton led his men against number 10 while a French column moved on number 9. The French prudently waited for their axemen to clear away brush, and for their caution they lost precious time and valuable men. Hamilton led his men quickly through ditches, bushes, and fallen trees. Suffering light casualties, they seized their objective and were evacuating British prisoners while the French were still struggling to secure redoubt number 9. Although Hamilton's exploits at Yorktown may not have been the most important military actions in the Revolution, he had at least proved to his adopted country, and to himself, that he was a capable soldier. The next day, Lieutenant Colonel Hamilton proudly sent this report of the engagement to Lafayette.

[Camp before Yorktown, Virginia,
October 15, 1781]

The American attack on Yorktown

Agreeable to your orders we advanced in two columns with unloaded arms, the right composed of Lt. Col [Jean-Joseph Sourbader de] Gimat's batalion and my own commanded by Major [Nicholas] Fish, the left of a detachment commanded by Lt Col [John] Laurens, destined to take the enemy in reverse, and intercept their retreat. The column on the right was preceded by a van guard of twenty men [led] by Lt. [John] Mansfield, and a detachment of sappers and miners, commanded by Capt [James] Gilliland for the purpose of removing obstructions.

The redoubt was commanded by Major [Patrick] Campbell, with a detachment of British and German troops, and was completely in a state of defence.

The rapidity and immediate success of the assault are the best comment on the behaviour of the troops. Lt Col Laurens distinguished himself by an exact and vigor-

Illumination.

COLONEL Tilghman, Aid de Camp to his Excellency General Washington, having brought official acounts of the SURRENDER of Lord Cornwallis, and the Garrifons of York and Gloucefter, thofe Citizens who chufe to ILLUMINATE on the Glorious Occasion, will do it this evening at Six, and extinguifh their lights at Nine o'clock.

Decorum and harmony are earneftly recommended to every Citizen, and a general difcountenance to the leaft appearance of riot.

October 24, 1781.

A broadside of 1781 announces an "illumination" to celebrate the American victory at Yorktown

ous execution of his part of the plan, by entering the enemy's work with his corps among the foremost, and making prisoner the commanding officer of the redoubt. Lt Col Gimat's batalion which formed the van of the right attack and which fell under my immediate observation, encouraged by the decisive and animated example of their leader, advanced with an ardor and resolution superior to every obstacle. They were well seconded by Major Fish with the batalion under his command, who when the front of the column reached the abatis, unlocking his corps to the left, as he had been directed, advanced with such celerity, as to arrive in time to participate in the assault. . . .

I do but justice to the several corps when I have the pleasure to assure you, there was not an officer nor soldier whose behaviour, if it could be particularized, would not have a claim to the warmest approbation. As it would have been attended with delay and loss to wait for the removal of the abatis and palisades the ardor of the troops was indulged in passing over them.

There was a happy coincidence of movements. The redoubt was in the same moment invelopped and carried on every part. The enemy are intitled to the acknowegement of an honorable defence. . . .

Our killed and wounded you will perceive by the inclosed return. I sensibly felt at a critical period the loss of the assistance of Lt. Col Gimat, who received a musket ball in his foot, which obliged him to retire from the field. . . .

Inclosed is a return of the prisoners. The killed and wounded of the enemy did not exceed eight. Incapable of imitating examples of barbarity, and forgetting recent provocations, the soldiery spared every man, who ceased to resist.

On October 19, Cornwallis surrendered his army of eight thousand men to the Americans. The Revolution was not yet over and many more American soldiers and French sailors would die in skirmishes and naval engagements before peace treaties were concluded. But the war had ended for Alexander Hamilton. He could now leave the Army with honor and join Betsey in Albany before the birth of their son, Philip, on January 22, 1782. At the end of February, Hamilton rode to Philadelphia to make his civilian status official. The Secretary of War, Benjamin Lincoln, had meantime requested that Hamilton be retained in the service because of "his superior abilities & knowledge." Hamilton, wishing to make his position clear, wrote to Washington offering a conditional resignation from active military duty.

[Philadelphia, March 1, 1782]

As I have many reasons to consider my being employed hereafter in a precarious light, the bare possibility of rendering an equivalent will not justify to my scruples the receiving any future emoluments from my commission. I therefore renounce from this time all claim to the compensations attached to my military station during the war or after it. But I have motives which will not permit me to resolve on a total resignation. I sincerely hope a prosperous train of affairs may continue to make it no inconvenience to decline the services of persons, whose zeal, in worse times, was found not altogether useless; but as the most promising appearances are often reversed by unforeseen disasters, and as unfortunate events may again make the same zeal of some value, I am unwilling to put it out of my power to renew my exertions in the common cause, in the line, in which I have hitherto acted. I shall accordingly retain my rank while I am permitted to do it, and take this opportunity to declare, that I shall be at all times ready to obey the call of the public, in any capacity civil, or military (consistent with what I owe to myself) in which there may be a prospect of my contributing to the final attainment of the object for which I embarked in the service.

Cornwallis surrenders to Washington and Rochambeau at Yorktown in this 1790 English engraving.

After Yorktown, America would most frequently call on Hamilton in his "civil" rather than his military capacity. Although Hamilton himself probably considered his service at Yorktown the most significant aspect of his life during 1780 and 1781, historians would quarrel with him. By accident or design, he had, in these two years, laid the foundation for his civilian career. By his marriage to Elizabeth Schuyler he had provided himself with a powerful political base in the state of New York. By his support of Army and congressional reform he had marked himself as a promising administrator and economic theorist. In the years of peace, few men would remember redoubt 10, but many would recall the perceptive comments of the young lieutenant colonel who had seen the flaws of the Confederation, and many would listen carefully when he repeated his arguments for political reform.

A Picture Portfolio

In Search of Military Glory

"I WISH THERE WAS A WAR"

In November, 1769, Alexander Hamilton wrote wistfully from St. Croix to his boyhood friend Ned Stevens in New York, saying, "I wish there was a war." The lad was not so much expressing a bellicose mood as he was dreaming of military glory—the only way a young man without an influential family or his own means could escape an unpromising future. Hamilton, of course, could not have known that the gathering storms of revolution would not only come to involve him but would also catapult him into the very center of the military action—and later would lead him into the political affairs of a new nation. While still at King's College in New York, Hamilton joined a volunteer company and "became exceedingly expert in the manual exercise." He then asked for the command of an artillery company, which the provincial congress authorized early in 1776, and he was duly appointed a captain at the age of twenty-one. Pictured at right in uniform, he was described by an older soldier as "a mere stripling, small slender, almost delicate in frame... with a cocked hat pulled down over his eyes...." In the actions that took place in New York and New Jersey during that desperate year, Hamilton came to the attention of General Washington, and on March 1, 1777, he was appointed to the Commander in Chief's staff (below) and commissioned a lieutenant colonel, a position he held for most of the next four years.

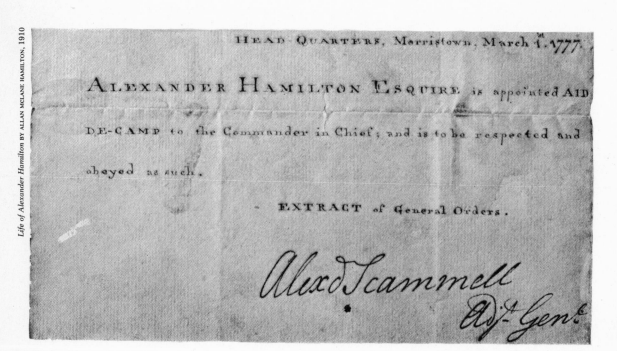

Life of Alexander Hamilton BY ALLAN MCLANE HAMILTON, 1910

HEAD-QUARTERS, Morristown, March 1, 1777.

ALEXANDER HAMILTON ESQUIRE is appointed AID

DE-CAMP to the Commander in Chief; and is to be respected and

obeyed as such.

EXTRACT of General Orders.

Alexd Scammell

Adjt Genl

HAMILTON TAKES A BRIDE

The brightest event of Hamilton's wartime service took place in the winter of 1779 when Betsey Schuyler (left) came to headquarters at Morristown, New Jersey, to visit her aunt. Daughter of the wealthy and influential Major General Philip Schuyler and his wife, Catherine Van Rensselaer Schuyler (left, above), the charming Betsey was eagerly courted by Hamilton. When they were married the following year, at her parents' home in Albany, he is thought to have presented her with the miniature by Charles Willson Peale above; the 1780 likeness is set in a highly decorative embroidered frame.

ARENAS OF COMBAT

Hamilton's two periods of significant combat in the Revolution came at the war's beginning and toward its end and in actual time amounted to slightly more than a year. As the Continental Army retreated through New Jersey in 1777, he was involved in the battles at Trenton and Princeton (below), and later at Monmouth. Major General Charles Lee, whom Washington had sent ahead at Monmouth, disobeyed orders; and when the Commander in Chief (at right on the black horse) came charging up to confront him, Hamilton and Lafayette (hatless) were right behind him. In Lee's subsequent court-martial Hamilton testified against him; while his closest friend, Lieutenant Colonel John Laurens (left), another aide who worshiped Washington, sought satisfaction with Lee in a duel in which Hamilton acted as his second. Neither man was wounded; but when Laurens was killed in combat five years later, Hamilton lost a valued confidant.

OVERLEAF:

At the war's climax, Hamilton again returned to military combat, successfully leading his troops in an attack on a British redoubt at Yorktown—a scene recorded in a panoramic painting by Eugene Lami.

A GLORIOUS FINALE

On October 19, 1781, the British surrendered at Yorktown and Alexander Hamilton's four years of military service at Washington's side ended. The day before, Cornwallis had sent a message to Washington proposing a cessation of hostilities for twenty-four hours and a meeting "at Mr. Moore's house [below], to settle terms for the surrender of the posts at York and Gloucester." Pleading illness, Cornwallis did not attend the surrender ceremony, and Washington appointed General Benjamin Lincoln to receive the surrender from Cornwallis's second-in-command. In the detail of John Trumbull's painting at left, Washington is astride the black horse, flanked by a number of his officers. Hamilton, in a position of honor he richly deserved, stands erect to the right of the gray horse, with his friend John Laurens beside him. Congress recognized Hamilton's contributions by adopting in January, 1782, a report citing his "superior abilities and knowledge of his profession" and including him among those officers to be retained in service. And Washington recognized Hamilton's worth by recalling him to his side several years later, naming him to his first Cabinet as Secretary of the Treasury. Hamilton's boyhood wish for a war had reaped a rich harvest.

Chapter 4

The War of Finance

In 1782, Alexander Hamilton found that for those men who shared his dreams for America the Revolution was only beginning. As an Army officer, he had grown dissatisfied with a government that let its troops go unfed, unclothed, and unpaid. As a civilian, he found himself in a circle of men dedicated to providing the United States with a peacetime government that would be more "respectable" and "energetic" than was the creaking, inefficient administrative machine that had hitherto directed America's affairs. This group of "nationalists" that fought to reform American government in 1782 and 1783 centered on the personality and policies of Robert Morris of Philadelphia. Appointed by Congress to head the Office of Finance, Morris chose as his assistant Gouverneur Morris, Hamilton's friend from New York days. Although the two Morrises were not related by blood, they were brothers in their determination to use the Office of Finance as a base for broader reform. While Hamilton was proving his military valor in the fall campaign of 1781, the Morrises were proving their worth as financial administrators by keeping the Army in the field. After Yorktown, they were ready to use their prestige to begin a wider program of financial policies that would strengthen the power and prestige of the national government.

In this "War of Finance," Alexander Hamilton was an obvious recruit for the Morrises' civilian "army" of men who believed that the American union could survive only if it was strong and efficient. Working first as an agent of the Office of Finance in New York and later as a member of Congress, Hamilton proved a courageous and daring warrior. The "impost," the "permanent fund," "half pay," "uniting the interest of the public creditors" — these were the battle cries of his campaign, and although they may sound strange today, they were part of a strategy as carefully thought out as any military expedition. Hamilton and the Morrises were determined to establish Continental revenues so that the national government would no longer have to make annual, often ignored, "requisitions" of funds from the states. By establishing an impost, a duty on imported goods, they hoped to set up a "permanent fund" for the payment of the public debt. By manipulating the Army's demands for "half-pay" pensions, they tried to unite the restless troops with the owners of government securities in hopes that this formidable body of public creditors might force the states to grant the impost and other "Continental" taxes. Eventually, however, Hamilton and his friends would go too far in their attempt to make the government work as they felt it must to preserve its independence. Hamilton's daring and dedication would turn to a recklessness and near fanaticism that was to damage the nationalist cause for years to come.

Originally, however, when he returned to his home in the spring of 1782, Hamilton had no plans other than to raise a family and to launch a private career that would enable him to support his wife and child. Shortly after his eldest son, Philip, was born in January, 1782, he wrote to his friend Richard Kidder Meade to disclaim interest in anything but the joys of family life—and the possibility of arranging a match between his infant son and Meade's newborn daughter.

> Philadelphia March 1782
>
> You cannot imagine how entirely domestic I am growing. I lose all taste for the pursuits of ambition, I sigh for nothing but the company of my wife and my baby. The ties of duty alone or imagined duty keep me from renouncing public life altogether. It is however probable I may not be any longer actively engaged in it....
>
> Betsy is so fond of your family that she proposes to form a match between her Boy & your girl provided you will engage to make the latter as amiable as her mother.
>
> Truly My Dear Meade, I often regret that fortune has cast our residence at such a distance from each other. It would be a serious addition to my happiness if we lived where I could see you every day but fate has determined it otherwise.

Domestic as he was, Hamilton could not resist a chance to express his views on public affairs. In the summer of 1781, four of his essays as "The Continentalist" had appeared in a Fishkill, New York, newspaper. In April, 1782, the fifth essay was published with this warning for Americans who resisted the policies of Congress and the Office of Finance.

> [Fishkill, New York, April 18, 1782]
>
> It is too much characteristic of our national temper to be ingenious in finding out and magnifying the minutest disadvantages, and to reject measures of evident utility even of necessity to avoid trivial and sometimes imaginary

evils. We seem not to reflect, that in human society, there is scarcely any plan, however salutary to the whole and to every part, by the share, each has in the common prosperity, but in one way, or another, and under particular circumstances, will operate more to the benefit of some parts, than of others. Unless we can overcome this narrow disposition and learn to estimate measures, by their general tendency, we shall never be a great or a happy people, if we remain a people at all.

Robert Morris needed men who would argue for his program, and "The Continentalist" only confirmed what he already knew of Alexander Hamilton's talents. In 1781, after he accepted his appointment from Congress as Superintendent of Finance, Morris had received a long letter of congratulations from the young colonel making it clear that they thought alike on financial and political matters. Accordingly, when Morris learned that Hamilton had left active military duty, he promptly offered him a post as "Receiver" of taxes, with responsibility for collecting New York's share of the eight million dollars requested from the states by Congress. Hamilton at first declined on the grounds that the salary for the office—25 per cent of taxes received—was not enough to allow him to take time from his legal studies in Albany. But when Morris assured him that his salary would be based on New York's full quota of taxes, whether or not that amount was actually collected, Hamilton wrote back accepting the appointment.

Hamilton's appointment as New York receiver of Continental taxes, signed and sealed by Robert Morris, 1782

[Albany, June 17, 1782]

In accepting it I have only one scruple, arising from a doubt whether the service I can render in the present state of things will be an equivalent for the compensation.... As the matter now stands there seems to be little for a Continental Receiver to do.... There is only one way in which I can imagine a prospect of being materially useful that is in seconding your applications to the State. In popular assemblies much may sometimes be brought about by personal discussions, by entering into details and combating objections as they rise. If it should at any time be thought adviseable by you to empower me to act in this capacity, I shall be happy to do every thing that depends on me to effectuate your views.

Robert Morris was only too happy to have Hamilton act as his lobbyist with the New York legislature, since that was precisely one of the roles he planned for his receivers. The young New Yorker shared

Morris's conviction that in the War of Finance, no chance should be lost for a useful skirmish with state assemblies. When the New York legislature was called into special session in July, 1782, to consider the problems of national finance, Hamilton set out to meet the lawmakers. But although the legislature was supposed to devote itself to "the Necessity of providing competent Means for a vigorous Prosecution of the War," after six days of conferences with a legislative committee, Hamilton had no encouraging news for Morris on revenue matters. However, he did see promise in a resolution passed by the legislature calling for a "general Convention" to amend the Confederation.

The high bluffs and rolling hills of the Poughkeepsie area, with Henry Livingston's estate and the Hudson River in the foreground

Poughkepsie [New York] July 22d. 1782

I think this a very eligible step though I doubt of the concurrence of the other states; but I am certain without it, they never will be brought to cooperate in any reasonable or effectual plan. Urge reforms or exertions and the answer constantly is what avails it for one state to make them without the concert of the others? It is in vain to expose the futility of this reasoning; it is founded on all those passions which have the strongest influence on the human mind.

The Legislature have also appointed at my instance a Committee to devise in the recess a more effectual system of taxation and to communicate with me on this subject. A good deal will depend on the success of this attempt. Convinced of the absurdity of multiplying taxes in the present mode, where in effect the payment is voluntary, and the money received exhausted in the collection, I have laboured chiefly to instil the necessity of a change in the plan, and though not so rapidly as the exigency of public affairs requires, truth seems to be making some progress.

Before the legislature adjourned, Hamilton was elected a New York delegate to the Continental Congress, his term to begin in November. This honor did nothing to help the young receiver collect taxes —or even to collect the statistics on state finances that Robert Morris demanded. As he waited, none too hopefully, for these "returns," Hamilton had time to prepare for Morris a "full view of the situation and temper" of New York. The scanty information that had come to the receiver's office convinced Hamilton that New York's finances were marked by an unfavorable balance of trade, which had caused "an *extreme* and *universal* scarcity of money." Local politics, he explained to the superintendent in his report, were no more encouraging.

The first session of America's
Continental Congress is depicted in
this French engraving, circa 1783.

Albany Augt. 13th. 1782

Here we find the general disease which infects all our constitutions, an excess of popularity. There is no *order* that has a will of its own. The inquiry constantly is what will *please* not what will *benefit* the people. In such a government there can be nothing but temporary expedient, fickleness and folly.

But the point of view in which this subject will be interesting to you is that which relates to our finances. I gave you in a former letter a sketch of our plan of taxation; but I will now be more particular.

The general principle of it is an assessment, according to *circumstances and abilities collectively considered.*

The ostensible reason for adopting this vague basis was a desire of equality: It was pretended, that this could not be obtained so well by any fixed tariff of taxable property, as by leaving it to the discretion of persons chosen by the people themselves, to determine the ability of each citizen. But perhaps the true reason was a desire to discriminate between the *whigs* and *tories.* This chimerical attempt at perfect equality has resulted in total inequality. . . .

The Legislature first *asseses,* or quotas the several counties. Here the evil begins. The members cabal and intrigue to throw the burthen off their respective constituents. Address and influence, more than considerations of real ability prevail. A great deal of time is lost and a great deal of expence incurred before the juggle is ended and the necessary compromises made.

The Supervisors . . . in each county, meet . . . and assign their proportions to the sub-divisions of the county; and in the distribution play over the same game, which was played in the Legislature.

The Assessors . . . according to their fancies, determine the proportion of each individual; a list of which [is] made out and . . . is a warrant to the collectors. . . .

It now remains for the collectors to collect the tax, and it is the duty of the supervisors to see that they do it. Both these offices . . . are elective; and of course there is little disposition to risk the displeasure of those who elect. . . .

You will perceive Sir, I have neither flattered the state nor encouraged high expectations. I thought it my duty to exhibit things as they are not as they ought to be. I shall be sorry, if it give an ill-opinion of the state for want of equal candor in the representations of others; for however disagreeable the reflection, I have too much reason to believe that the true picture of other states would be in proportion to their circumstances equally unpromising. All my inquiries and all that appears induces this opinion. I intend this letter *in confidence to yourself* and therefore I indorse it *private.*

In the last week of August, Hamilton received urgent appeals for cash from Philadelphia but continued to get only evasions and excuses from New York authorities. Two months as a Continental receiver had only confirmed his cynicism about his fellow citizens. Writing to Richard Kidder Meade from Albany, Hamilton shared his thoughts on mankind, his seven-month-old son, and his plans for the future.

Albany Augt 27th. 1782

Experience is a continued comment on the worthlessness of the human race and the few exceptions we find have the greater right to be valued in proportion as they are rare. I know few men estimable, fewer amiable & when I meet with one of the last description it is not in my power to withhold my affection.

You reproach me with not having said enough about our little stranger. When I wrote last I was not sufficiently acquainted with him to give you his character. I may now assure you that your daughter when she sees him will not consult you about the choice or will only do it in respect to the rules of decorum. He is truly a very fine young gentleman, the most agreable in his conversation and manners of any I ever knew — nor less remarkable for his intelligence and sweetness of temper. You are not to imagine by my beginning with his mental qualifications that he is defective in personal. It is agreed on all hands, that he is handsome, his features are good, his eye is not only sprightly and expressive but it is full of benignity. His attitude in sitting is by connoisseurs esteemed graceful and he has a method of waving his hand that announces the future orator. He stands however rather awkwardly and his legs have not all the delicate slimness of his fathers. It is feared He may never excel as much in dancing which is probably the only accomplishment in which he will not be a model. If he has any fault in manners, he laughs too much. He has now passed his Seventh

Month....

As to myself I shall sit down in New York when it opens & the period we are told approaches. No man looks forward to a Peace with more pleasure than I do, though no man would sacrifice less to it than myself, If I were not convinced the people sigh for peace. I have been studying the Law for some months and have lately been licenced as an attorney. I wish to prepare myself by October for Examination as a Counsellor but some public avocations may possibly prevent me.

I had almost forgotten to tell you, that I have been ... elected ... a member of Congress.... I do not hope to reform the State although I shall endeavour to do all the good I can.

*A five-hundred-dollar bond issued
by the Continental treasury in 1781*

The New York legislature had named a special committee on taxation, which was to meet on September 15, 1782. The committee's sessions offered Hamilton a last chance to make a contribution as a receiver, since he would have to resign this post to take his seat in Congress in November. But, as he reported to Robert Morris on October 5, the committee did little.

[Albany, October 5, 1782]
In spite of my efforts, they have parted without doing any thing decisive. They have indeed agreed upon several matters and those of importance but they have not reduced them to the form of a report, which in fact leave every thing afloat to be governed by the impressions of the moment when the legislature meet.

The points agreed upon are these—that there shall be an actual valuation of land and a tax of so much in the pound.... That there shall be also a tariff of all personal property to be also taxed at so much in the pound—that there shall be a specific tax on carriages clocks watches & other similar articles of luxury—that money at usury shall be taxed at a fixed rate in the pound excluding that which is loand to the public—that houses in all towns shall be taxed at a certain proportion of the annual rent —that there shall be a poll tax on all single men from fifteen upwards and that the Collection of the taxes should be advertised to the lowest bidder at a fixed rate P[er] Cent bearing all subordinate expences.

Among other things which were rejected I pressed hard for an excise on distilled liquors; but all that could be carried on these articles was a license on taverns.

The Committee were pretty generally of opinion that the system of funding for payment of old debts & for procuring further credit was wise & indispensable but a majority thought it would be unwise in one state to contribute in this way alone.

Nothing was decided on the quantum of taxes which the state was able to pay; those who went furthest would not exceed 70000 £ of which fifty for the use of the United states.

When Hamilton was elected to Congress in the summer of 1782, he showed some guarded enthusiasm for the idea of carrying on the War of Finance in Philadelphia. Further encouraged by news of peace negotiations in Europe, he tried to recruit his friend John Laurens for the finance campaign.

[Albany, August 15, 1782]
Your wishes in one respect are gratified; this state has pretty unanimously delegated me to Congress. My time of service commences in November.... We have great reason to flatter ourselves peace on our own terms is upon the carpet....

I fear there may be obstacles but I hope they may be surmounted.

Peace made, My Dear friend, a new scene opens. The object then will be to make our independence a blessing. To do this we must secure our *union* on solid foundations; an herculean task and to effect which mountains of prejudice must be levelled!

It requires all the virtue and all the abilities of the Country. Quit your sword my friend, put on the *toga*, come to Congress. We know each others sentiments, our views are the same: we have fought side by side to make America free, let us hand in hand struggle to make her happy.

YALE UNIVERSITY ART GALLERY

Hamilton (left) and his friend John Laurens appear in this detail from Trumbull's painting of the British surrender at Yorktown.

Laurens probably never read his friend's letter. On August 27, he was killed in a skirmish with British troops at Combahee Ferry, South Carolina. Hamilton was stunned by the news. He had always been reluctant to give his trust or friendship to any man, and Laurens had gained his confidence and affection completely. In mid-October, Hamilton tried to explain his feelings to Nathanael Greene.

[Albany, October 12, 1782]

I feel the deepest affliction at the news we have just received of the loss of our dear and inestimable friend Laurens. His career of virtue is at an end. How strangely are human affairs conducted, that so many excellent qualities could not ensure a more happy fate? The world will feel the loss of a man who has left few like him behind, and America of a citizen whose heart realized that patriotism of which others only talk. I feel the loss of a friend I truly and most tenderly loved, and one of a very small number.

As Hamilton prepared for his trip to Philadelphia, he found that he had lost much of his zest for Continental service. With his closest friend dead, he was forced to leave his wife and child at a time when he needed the security of his family most. It is not surprising that he insisted to Lafayette that he was "already tired" of public life.

Gouverneur Morris

[Albany, November 3, 1782]

I have been employed for the last ten months in rocking the cradle and studying the art of fleecing my neighbours. I am now a Grave Counsellor at law, and shall soon be a grand member of Congress.... I am going to throw away a few months more in public life and then I retire a simple citizen and good paterfamilias. I set out for Philadelphia in a few days. You see the disposition I am in. You are condemned to run the race of ambition all your life. I am already tired of the career and dare to leave it.

But you would not give a pin for my letter unless politics or war made a part of it. You tell me they are employed in building *a peace*; And other accounts say it is nearly finished; I hope the work may meet with no interruptions: it is necessary for America; especially if your army is taken from us as we are told will soon be the case.... These states are in no humour for continuing exertions; if the war lasts, it must be carried on by external succours. I make no apology for the inertness of this country. I detest it; but since it exists I am sorry to see other resources diminish.

Once Hamilton had taken his seat in Congress, his interest in public affairs revived quickly. There he found other men, including Robert and Gouverneur Morris and James Madison, a young congressman from Virginia, who were as eager as he was to press for reform. The most urgent problem facing them in the winter of 1782–83 was the fate of the Continental duty on imports. Under the Articles of Confederation, the impost could not go into effect without the consent of all thirteen states. By November, 1782, only Rhode Island still withheld its approval. Shortly before Hamilton took his seat on November 25, Congress received unofficial word that Rhode Island had flatly rejected the impost. At Hamilton's suggestion, Congress voted to send a delegation to Rhode Island to plead for the import duty. On December 11, Hamilton presented a draft letter for the delegation to deliver to Governor William Greene in Providence.

Philadelphia [December 11, 1782]
Congress are equally affected and alarmed by the information they have received that the Legislature of your state at their last meeting have refused their concurrence in the establishment of a duty on imports. They consider this measure as so indispensable to the prosecution of the war, that a sense of duty and regard to the common safety compel them to renew their efforts to engage a compliance with it; and in this view they have determined to send a deputation of three of their members to your state.... The Gentlemen they have appointed will be able to lay before you a full and just representation of the public affairs....

They will only briefly observe that the increasing discontents of the army, the loud clamours of the public creditors, and the extreme disproportion between the current supplies and the demands of the public service are so many invincible arguments for the fund recommended by Congress. They feel themselves unable to devise any other, that will be more efficacious, less exceptionable or more generally agreeable; and if this is rejected they anticipate calamities of a most menacing nature, with this consolation however, that they have faithfully discharged their trust, and that the mischiefs which may follow cannot be attributed to them.

Robert Morris, by Peale

Before the delegation could depart for Rhode Island with Hamilton's carefully drafted message, Congress received a harsh letter from William Bradford, speaker of the state's assembly. Confirming the legislature's veto of the impost, Bradford remarked that Rhode Island would cease to "suspect the virtue of the present Congress" only when Congress's resolutions were "founded on the great principles of liberty, and a general interest." Hamilton, Madison, and Thomas FitzSimons of Pennsylvania were named to prepare a reply to the speaker's letter. Their report, almost wholly Hamilton's work, closed with a stinging rebuttal.

[Philadelphia] December 16, 1782

It is certainly pernicious to leave any government in a situation of responsibility, disproportioned to its power.

The conduct of the war is intrusted to Congress and the public expectation turned upon them without any competent means at their command to satisfy the important trust. After the most full and solemn deliberation under a collective view of all the public difficulties, they recommend a measure, which appears to them the corner stone of the public safety: They see this measure suspended for near two years—partially complied with by some of the states, rejected by one of them and in danger on that account to be frustrated; the public embarrassments every day increasing, the dissatisfaction of the army growing more serious, the other creditors of the public clamouring for justice, both irritated by the delay of measures for their present relief or future security, the hopes of our enemies encouraged to protract the war, the zeal of our friends depressed by an appearance of remissness and want of exertion, on our part, Congress harrassed, the national character suffering and the national safety at the mercy of events.

William Bradford

By December, 1782, one group of public creditors had become especially anxious for settlement of its claims. As the conclusion of a peace treaty now seemed imminent, Army officers and enlisted men were beginning to wonder whether they would be reimbursed for back pay and other expenses. On December 31, the same day that Congress learned that Virginia had withdrawn its approval of the impost, a delegation from the Army at West Point arrived in Philadelphia to petition Congress for the back pay and half-pay pensions that had been promised to officers. This coincidence gave a new turn to nationalist strategy, as Hamilton hinted in a letter to Governor George Clinton.

Philda. [January 12] 1783

We have now here a deputation from the army, and feel a mortification of a total disability to comply with their just expectations. If, however, the matter is taken up in a proper manner, I think their application may be turned to a good account. Every day proves more & more the insufficiency of the confederation. The proselytes to this opinion are increasing fast....

Hamilton and Madison, named to consider the Army petition, clearly demonstrated the "turn" to which military claims could be put. They argued that the half-pay pensions might be paid in government securities, which would be supported, of course, by a permanent fund provided by the impost. The Army delegates, headed by Hamilton's old friend General Alexander McDougall, gave added weight to the nationalists' argument by testifying that the Army might react violently if its claims were ignored. To back up the general's testimony another of Hamilton's friends, Colonel John Brooks, returned to camp in mid-February to report to his fellow officers on the mood of Congress, and apparently to encourage some sort of concrete demonstration of military unrest. In the meantime, Hamilton sent Washington the following outline of the role he expected the Commander to play in the finance campaign. A similar proposal was sent by Gouverneur Morris and Alexander McDougall to General Henry Knox.

[Philadelphia, February 13, 1783]

If the war continues it would seem that the army must in June subsist itself *to defend the* country; if peace should take place it *will* subsist itself to *procure justice to itself.* It appears to be a prevailing opinion in the army that the disposition to recompence their services will cease with the necessity for them, and that if they once lay down their arms, they will part with the means of obtaining justice. It is to be lamented that appearances afford too much ground for their distrust.

It becomes a serious inquiry what will be the true line of policy. The claims of the army urged with moderation, but with firmness, may operate on those weak minds which are influenced by their apprehensions more than their judgments; so as to produce a concurrence in the measures which the exigencies of affairs demand. They may add weight to the applications of Congress to the several states. So far an useful turn may be given to them. But the difficulty will be to keep a *complaining* and *suffering army* within the bounds of moderation....

[Hamilton had come to the point. Washington was to control the Army's protests and advance the cause of Continental financial policies.]

This Your Excellency's influence must effect. In order to [do] it, it will be adviseable not to discountenance their endeavours to procure redress, but rather by the intervention of confidential and prudent persons, *to take the direction of them.* This however must not appear: it is

WAR DEPARTMENT COLLECTION, NATIONAL ARCHIVES

Soldiers in the Continental Army were reimbursed for back pay with "final Settlement" certificates signed by Paymaster John Pierce.

of moment to the public tranquillity that Your Excellency should preserve the confidence of the army without losing that of the people. This will enable you in case of extremity to guide the torrent, and bring order perhaps even good, out of confusion. 'Tis a part that requires address; but 'tis one which your own situation as well as the welfare of the community points out.

I will not conceal from Your Excellency a truth which it is necessary you should know. An idea is propagated in the army that delicacy carried to an extreme prevents your espousing its interests with sufficient warmth. The falsehood of this opinion no one can be better acquainted with than myself; but it is not the less mischievous for being false. Its tendency is to impair that influence, which you may exert with advantage, should any commotions unhappily ensue, to moderate the pretensions of the army and make their conduct correspond with their duty.

The great *desideratum* at present is the establishment of general funds, which alone can do justice to the Creditors of the United States (of whom the army forms the most meritorious class), restore public credit and supply the future wants of government. This is the object of all men of sense; in this the influence of the army, properly directed, may cooperate.

United States History, LOSSING

Washington's headquarters at Newburgh, New York

A week after Colonel Brooks's departure for West Point there was still no word of Army unrest and still no answer from Washington or Henry Knox. Nevertheless, the nationalists continued their campaign in Philadelphia, pressing their fight for the impost and insisting that the Army was near mutiny. On the evening of February 20, at a private conference, Hamilton and Richard Peters, Secretary of the Board of War, gave their version of the "temper, transactions & views of the army." James Madison, who took notes during the meeting, left a record of their remarks.

[Philadelphia, February 20, 1783]

Mr. Hamilton & Mr. Peters... informed the company that the army had secretly determined not to lay down their arms until due provision & a satisfactory prospect should be afforded on the subject of their pay; that there was reason to expect that a public declaration to this effect would soon be made; that plans had been agitated if not formed for subsisting themselves after such declaration; that as a proof of their earnestness on this subject the Commander was already become extremely unpopular

Colonel Walter Stewart

among almost all ranks from his known dislike to every unlawful proceeding, that this unpopularity was daily increasing & industriously promoted by many leading characters....Mr. Hamilton said that he knew Genl. Washington intimately and perfectly, that his extreme reserve, mixed sometimes with a degree of asperity of temper both of which were said to have increased of late, had contributed to the decline of his popularity; but that his virtue his patriotism & his firmness would it might be depended upon never yield to any dishonorable or disloyal plans into which he might be called; that he would sooner suffer himself to be cut into pieces; that he, (Mr. Hamilton) knowing this to be his true character wished him to be the conductor of the army in their plans for redress, in order that they might be moderated & directed to proper objects, & exclude some other leader who might foment and misguide their councils; that with this view he had taken the liberty to write to the Genl. on this subject and to recommend such a policy to him.

By the beginning of March it was clear that John Brooks's mission had failed and that neither Knox nor Washington would become involved in a plan to use the Army for political purposes. Time was running out for the nationalists. There were now unofficial reports that a provisional peace treaty had been signed, and it was obvious that the states would be reluctant to establish permanent funds once hostilities were ended. From New York, however, came encouraging news. At Army headquarters in Newburgh, a group of officers led by Colonel Walter Stewart, who had just arrived from Philadelphia to assume his duties as an Inspector of the Army, had begun circulating the "Newburgh Addresses," which attacked Congress and the Commander in Chief and warned that the Army would not lay down its arms until its claims were met. There is no evidence that Hamilton or the Morrises had any connection with Stewart, although their opponents believed otherwise. When Washington wrote to Hamilton demanding to know what part the nationalists had played in the budding revolt, Hamilton sent him this reply.

Philadelphia, March 17. 1783
Your Excellency mentions that it has been surmised the plan in agitation was formed in Philadelphia; that combinations have been talked of between the public creditors and the army; and that members of Congress had incouraged the idea. This is partly true. I have myself urged in Congress the propriety of uniting the influence

of the public creditors, & the army as a part of them, to prevail upon the states to enter into their views. I have expressed the same sentiments out of doors. Several other members of Congress have done the same. The meaning however of all this was simply that Congress should adopt such a plan as would embrace the relief of all the public creditors including the army; in order that the personal influence of some, the connections of others, and a sense of justice to the army as well as the apprehension of ill consequences might form a mass of influence in each state in favour of the measures of Congress. In this view, as I mentioned to Your Excellency in a former letter, I thought the discontents of the army might be turned to a good account. I am still of opinion that their earnest, but respectful applications for redress will have a good effect.

As to any combination of *Force* it would only be productive of the horrors of a civil war, might end in the ruin of the Country & would certainly end in the ruin of the army.

For a time it seemed as if the nationalist gamble might pay off. While quelling the mutiny, Washington was able to turn the occasion into a stirring reaffirmation of the Army's sense of honor and duty, and on March 21, Hamilton reintroduced a plan for half pay to Congress. But events were moving too fast for Hamilton and his friends. Prospects for a settlement with the Army or the creation of a permanent fund grew dimmer when, on March 24, the preliminary treaty of peace between Britain and the Allies was read in Congress. A few days later Washington received Hamilton's candid appraisal of the Army's chances of receiving justice either from Congress or the states.

Phila. Mar 25th 1783

Here I write as a citizen zealous for the true happiness of this country, as a soldier who feels what is due to an army which has suffered everything and done much for the safety of America.

I sincerely wish *ingratitude* was not so natural to the human heart as it is. I sincerely wish there were no seeds of it in those who direct the councils of the United States. But while I urge the army to moderation, and advise Your Excellency to take the direction of their discontents, and endeavour to confine them within the bounds of duty, I cannot as an honest man conceal from you, that I am afraid their distrusts have too much foundation. Republican jealousy has in it a principle of hostility to an army whatever be their merits, whatever be their claims to the gratitude of the community. It acknowleges their services with unwillingness and rewards them with reluctance. I see this temper, though smothered with great care, involuntarily breaking out upon too many occasions. I often feel a mortification, which it would be impolitic to express, that sets my passions at variance with my reason. Too many I perceive, if they could do it with safety or colour, would be glad to elude the just pretensions of the army. I hope that this is not the prevailing disposition.

But supposing the Country ungrateful what can the army do? It must submit to its hard fate. To seek redress by its arms would end in its ruin. The army would moulder by its own weight and for want of the means of keeping together. The soldiery would abandon their officers. There would be no chance of success without having recourse to means that would reverse our revolution. I make these observations not that I imagine Your Excellency can want motives to continue your influence in the path of moderation; but merely to show why I cannot myself enter into the views of coertion which some Gentlemen entertain, for I confess could force avail I should almost wish to see it employed. I have an indifferent opinion of the honesty of this country, and ill-forebodings as to its future system.

Your Excellency will perceive I have written with sensations of chagrin and will make allowance for colouring; but the general picture is too true.

God send us all more wisdom.

An English engraving of the signing of the preliminary peace treaty between Britain and the Allies

When Washington replied, Hamilton felt even more "chagrin," for it was apparent that the Commander had not accepted his version of the history of the Newburgh "Conspiracy." Many officers, Washington wrote Hamilton, had become convinced that "some members" of Congress had intended to use the Army "as mere Puppets to establish Continental funds" and would "make a sacrafice of the Army and all its interests" to win these revenues. Hamilton replied promptly—if not too honestly.

[Philadelphia, April 8, 1783]

I do not wonder at the suspicions that have been infused, nor should I be surprised to hear that I have been pointed out as one of the persons concerned in playing the game described. But facts must speak for themselves. The Gentlemen who were here from the army; General Mc. Dougall who is still here will be able to give a true account of those who have supported the just claims of the army, and of those who have endeavoured to elude them.

There are two classes of men Sir in Congress of very Different views—one attached to state, the other to Continental politics. The last have been strenuous advocates for funding the public debt upon solid securities, the former have given every opposition in their power and have only been dragged into the measures which are now near being adopted by the clamours of the army and other public creditors. The advocates for Continental funds have blended the interests of the army with other Creditors from a conviction, that no funds for partial purposes will go through those states to whose citizens the United States are largely indebted—or if they should be carried through from impressions of the moment would have the necessary stability; for the influence of those unprovided for would always militate against a provision for others, in exclusion of them. It is in vain to tell men who have parted with a large part of their property on the public faith that the services of the army are intitled to a preference. They would reason from their interest and their feelings. These would tell them that they had as great a title as any other class of the community to public justice, and that while this was denied to them, it would be unreasonable to make them bear their part of a burthen for the benefit of others. This is the way they would reason & as their influence in some of the states was considerable they would have been able to prevent any partial provision. . . .

[Hamilton then described the tactics of the opposing groups in Congress with regard to commutation and pensions.]

The opinions on this head have been two. One party was for referring the several lines to their states to make such commutation as they should think proper—the other for making the commutation by Congress and funding it on continental security. I was of this last opinion and so were all those who will be represented as having made

The Commander in Chief, General Washington, in a 1782 engraving

use of the army as puppets. Our principal reasons were 1st by referring the lines to their respective states, those which were opposed to the half pay would have taken advantage of the officers necessities, to make the commutation far short of an equivalent. 2dly. The inequality which would have arisen in the different states when the officers came to compare... would have been a new source of discontent. 3dly. such a reference was a continuance of the old wretched state system, by which the ties between Congress and the army have been nearly dissolved—by which the resources of the states have been diverted from the common treasury & wasted; a system which Your Excellency has often justly reprobated.

...I assure you upon my honor Sir I have given you a candid state of facts to the best of my judgment. The men against whom the suspicions you mention must be directed are in general the most sensible the most liberal, the most independent and the most respectable characters in our body as well as the most unequivocal friends to the army. In a word they are the men who think continentally.

Hamilton had been half right in predicting that the outcome of the "storm" at Newburgh would "add new lustre" to the Army's "character" and "strengthen the hands of Congress." Congress reaffirmed the Government's commitment to half pay, but refused to listen to Hamilton's pleas for strong, nationalist tax measures. On April 18, a new impost was recommended to the states, but this time the provision for the import duty was so watered down that Hamilton could not bring himself to vote for the revenue measure—even though it was earmarked for the payment of the public debt. A month later, Hamilton outlined his reasons for opposing the new impost to Governor Clinton.

Philadelphia May 14 1783

1st That it does not designate the funds (except the impost) on which the whole interest is to arise; and by which ...the collection would have been easy, the fund productive and necessarily increasing with the increase of the Country.

2dly. That the duration of the fund is not coextensive with the debt but limited to twenty five years, though there is a moral certainty that in that period, the principal will not by the present provision be fairly extinguished.

3dly That the nomination and appointment of the collectors of the revenue are to reside in each state . . . the consequence of which will be, that those states which have little interest in the fund by having a small share of the public debt due to their own citizens will take care to appoint such persons as are least likely to collect the revenue.

The evils resulting from these defects will be that in many instances the objects of the revenues will be improperly chosen and will . . . on experiment prove insufficient — that for want of a vigorous collection in each state, the revenue will be unproductive in many and will fall chiefly upon those states which are governed by most liberal principles; that for want of an adequate security, the evidences of the public debt will not be transferrable for anything like their value — that this . . . will deprive the public of the benefit of an increased circulation, and of course will disable the people from paying the taxes for want of a sufficient medium. . . .

[Although Hamilton declared he would be "happy" if his gloomy predictions were proved false, he made it clear that he did not expect that he would have to admit any error in judgment.]

I hope our state will consent to the plan proposed; because it is her interest at all events to promote the payment of the public debt on Continental funds (independent of the general considerations of Union & propriety). I am much mistaken if the debts due from the United States to the citizens of the state of New York do not considerably exceed its proportion of the necessary funds, of course it has an immediate interest that there should be a Continental provision for them. But there are superior motives that ought to operate in every state, the obligations of national faith honor and reputation.

Individuals have been already too long sacrificed to public convenience. It will be shocking and indeed an eternal reproach to this country, if we begin the peaceable enjoyment of our independence by a violation of all the principles of honesty & true policy. . . .

P. S. It is particularly interesting that the state should have a representation here. Not only many matters are depending which require a full representation in Congress and there is now a thin one; but those matters are

A view of the Philadelphia State House, as it appeared in 1778

of a nature so particularly interesting to our state, that we ought not to be without a voice in them. I wish two other Gentlemen of the delegation may appear as soon as possible for it would be very injurious to me to remain much longer here. Having no future view in public life, I owe it to myself without delay to enter upon the care of my private concerns in earnest.

As the last lines of this letter suggest, Hamilton was now more than ready to end his career in the wartime Congress. He outlined his plans and his complaints in a letter to Nathanael Greene.

[Philadelphia, June 10, 1783]
I expect to leave this shortly for that place [Albany] and to remain there 'till New York is evacuated [by the British]; on which event I shall set down there seriously on the business of making my fortune....

There is so little disposition either in or out of Congress to give solidity to our national system that there is no motive to a man to lose his time in the public service; who has no other view than to promote its welfare. Experience must convince us that our present establishments are Utopian before we shall be ready to part with them for better.

Soon, however, the discontents of the Army forced Hamilton to change his plans for returning to New York. Soldiers from the regiment stationed at Lancaster, Pennsylvania, had begun a march on Philadelphia to demand a settlement of their accounts, and Hamilton was named to a congressional committee that was to confer with the Executive Council of the State of Pennsylvania on measures for dealing with the mutinous troops. On the afternoon of June 21, several hundred angry, unpaid members of the Continental Army surrounded the State House to demand a hearing from Congress. Hamilton reported to Congress on his committee's meetings with state authorities on June 22 and June 23.

[Philadelphia] June 24, 1783
The Committee ... beg leave to report:
That the Council had a high respect for the representative sovereignty of the United States and were disposed to do every thing in their power to support its dignity. That they regretted the insult which had happened.... That they had consulted a number of well-informed officers of the militia, and found that nothing in the

present state of things was to be expected from that quarter. That the Militia of the city in general were not only ill provided for service, but disinclined to act upon the present occasion. That the Council did not believe any exertions were to be looked for from them, except in case of further outrage and actual violence to person and property. That in such a case a respectable body of citizens would arm for the security of their property and of the public peace; but it was to be doubted what measure of outrage would produce this effect; and in particular it was not to be expected merely from a repetition of the insult which had happened. . . .

[When the council declared that a "policy of coertion" against the rebellious troops was unnecessary, Hamilton's committee replied indignantly.]

That the excesses of the mutineers had passed those bounds within which a spirit of compromise might consist with the dignity and even the safety of government. That impunity for what had happened might encourage to more flagrant proceedings, invite others to follow the example and extend the mischief. . . . That these considerations had determined Congress to adopt decisive measures. That . . . they had not neglected other means of ultimately executing their purpose but had directed the Commander in Chief to march a detachment of troops towards the city. That whatever moderation it might be prudent to exercise towards the mutineers, when they were once in the power of government it was necessary in the first instance to place them in that situation. That Congress would probably continue to persue this object unless it should be superseded by unequivocal demonstrations of submission on the part of the mutineers. That they had hitherto given no satisfactory evidence of this disposition, having lately presented the officers they had chosen to represent their grievances with a formal commission in writing, enjoining them if necessary to use compulsory means for redress, and menacing them with death in case of their failing to execute their views. . . .

The Committee finding that there was no satisfactory ground to expect prompt and adequate exertions on the part of the Executive of this state . . . were bound by the resolution under which they acted to advice the president to summon Congress to assemble at Princeton or Trenton on Thursday.

Congress beat an undignified and hasty retreat to Princeton, New Jersey, leaving the mutineers to the authorities in Philadelphia. By this time, Hamilton was growing more and more anxious to end his term in Congress—a legislature that could neither provide for the Army that had won American independence, nor raise funds to pay the nation's debts, nor even insure the safety of the building in which it assembled. Still, Hamilton had enough faith in the body to prepare a lengthy resolution enumerating the defects of the Articles of Confederation and calling for a convention to amend the articles. He began by listing "essential points" in which the confederation was "defective."

Hamilton's letter informing Governor Clinton that Congress had removed to Princeton to avoid mutineers from the Army barracks in Philadelphia

[Princeton, New Jersey, July, 1783]

First and generally in confining the power of the fœderal government within too narrow limits, withholding from it that efficacious authority and influence in all matters of general concern which are indispensable to the harmony and welfare of the whole—embarrassing general provisions by unnecessary details and inconvenient exceptions incompatible with their nature tending only to create jealousies and disputes respecting the proper bounds of the authority of the United States and of that of the particular states, and a mutual interference of the one with the other.

Secondly. In confounding legislative and executive powers in a single body . . . contrary to the most approved and well founded maxims of free government which require that the legislative executive and judicial authorities should be deposited in distinct and separate hands.

Thirdly. In the want of a Fœderal Judicature having cognizance of all matters of general concern in the last resort, especially those in which foreign nations, and their subjects are interested; from which defect, by the interference of the local regulations of particular states militating directly or indirectly against the powers vested in the Union, the national treaties will be liable to be infringed, the national faith to be violated and the public tranquillity to be disturbed. . . .

[After listing seven more specific ways in which the Articles of Confederation failed to provide for America's interests in finance, trade, and national security, Hamilton turned to broader defects in the system.]

11thly. In requiring the assent of *nine* states to matters of principal importance and of seven to all others...a rule destructive of vigour, consistency or expedition in the administration of affairs, tending to subject the *sense* of the majority to *that* of the minority...the evils of which...must always make the spirit of government, a spirit of compromise and expedient, rather than of system and energy.

12thly. In vesting in the Fœderal government the sole direction of the interests of the United States in their intercourse with foreign nations, without empowering it to pass all general laws in aid and support of the laws of nations; for the want of which authority, the faith of the United States may be broken, their reputation sullied, and their peace interrupted by the negligence or misconception of any particular state.

[Having completed his analysis of the faults of the present Government, Hamilton closed his "Resolution" with his proposals for a remedy.]

And Whereas it is essential to the happiness and security of these states, that their union, should be established on the most solid foundations, and it is manifest that this desireable object cannot be effected but by a government capable both in peace and war of making every member of the Union contribute in just proportion to the common necessities, and of combining and directing the forces and wills of the several parts to a general end; to which purposes in the opinion of Congress the present confederation is altogether inadequate.

And Whereas on the spirit which may direct the councils and measures of these states at the present juncture may depend their future safety and welfare; Congress conceive it to be their duty freely to state to their constituents the defects which by experience have been discovered in the present plan of the Fœderal Union and solemnly to call their attention to a revisal and amendment of the same:

Therefore Resolved that it be earnestly recommended to the several states to appoint a convention to meet...

Adams, Morris, Hamilton, and Jefferson are shown conferring at the Continental Congress.

with full powers to revise the confederation and to adopt and propose such alterations as to them shall appear necessary to be finally approved or rejected by the states respectively—and that a Committee...be appointed to prepare an address upon the subject.

Congress never heard this draft resolution for a convention; the manuscript carries Hamilton's terse notation: "abandoned for want of support." Finally, at the end of July, 1783, Hamilton left Congress. His mood at the time was best expressed in a letter he sent to his old friend John Jay, one of the commissioners who had negotiated America's treaty of peace with Britain.

[Philadelphia, July 25, 1783]
We have now happily concluded the great work of independence, but much remains to be done to reach the fruits of it. Our prospects are not flattering. Every day proves the inefficacy of the present confederation, yet the common danger being removed, we are receding instead of advancing in a disposition to amend its defects. The road to popularity in each state is to inspire jealousies of the power of Congress, though nothing can be more apparent than that they have no power; and that for the want of it, the resources of the country during the war could not be drawn out, and we at this moment experience all the mischiefs of a bankrupt and ruined credit. It is to be hoped that when prejudice and folly have run themselves out of breath we may return to reason and correct our errors.

Hamilton returned gladly to the joys of raising a family and the challenge of building a law practice in New York. It was a fortunate decision both for him and for the nation he had tried to serve. By July, 1783, the American public and Hamilton needed a rest from the strain of eight years of war and revolution. Since 1775, Hamilton's fellow citizens had undergone political upheaval, economic hardship, and military danger; there was little national energy left for the "exertions" Hamilton and other nationalists had demanded. For his part, Hamilton, in his desire to introduce reforms, had lost his sense of perspective about the role of a public servant in a republic. If he was to serve America, he first had to learn more about that nation. A few quiet years as a New York lawyer would permit him to observe his neighbors more closely. When he returned to public life, he would not repeat his mistakes of 1783.

Chapter **5**

Devil's Advocate

When Alexander Hamilton returned to New York in August, 1783, he might have sincerely believed that he could pursue his private career without troubling himself with public affairs. But he soon learned that a conscientious nationalist could not even earn a living without confronting flaws of government and threats to the nation's "character." One of the most bothersome issues involved New York's reaction to the provisions of the Treaty of Paris, under which Britain and the United States had agreed that neither nation would permit the persecution of any persons for the part they had taken in the war. New Yorkers showed no inclination to end such actions. Beginning in 1779 with the Confiscation Act, under which "attainted" Loyalists forfeited their property, the state legislature had enacted a series of harsh laws against British sympathizers. Under the Trespass Act of 1783, New Yorkers who had fled from their homes could bring action against those who had remained behind British lines and occupied their property.

This list of laws brought Hamilton a harvest of legal fees. In all, he handled at least forty-five cases under the Trespass Act and twenty more under other anti-Loyalist laws. But although Hamilton's success in many of these trials won him a reputation as an able and resourceful attorney, he was too concerned with the nation's "character" to view the treaty violations with anything but disgust. He knew that the continued enforcement of these laws might endanger America's national prestige. In June, 1783, when he was still serving New York in the Continental Congress, Hamilton had written to Governor George Clinton expressing his concern about his home state's refusal to comply with the treaty's provisions. Hamilton pointed out that since the preliminary articles of peace had not yet been ratified, New York's violations of the treaty might give Britain an excuse to postpone complying with other provisions of the agreement.

Philadelphia June 1st 1783

...with a treaty which has exceeded the hopes of the

most sanguine...I think it the height of imprudence to run any risk. Great Britain without recommencing hostilities may evade parts of the treaty. She may keep possession of the frontier posts, she may obstruct the free enjoyment of the fisheries, she may be indisposed to such extensive concessions in matters of commerce as it is our interest to aim at; in all this she would find no opposition from any foreign power; and we are not in a condition to oblige her to any thing. If we imagine that France, obviously embarrassed herself in her Finances would renew the war to oblige Great Britain to the restoration of our frontier posts, or to a compliance with the stipulations respecting the fisheries...we speculate much at random....Are we prepared, for the mere gratification of our resentments to put those great national objects to the hazard—to leave our western frontier in a state of insecurity—to relinquish the fur trade and to abridge our pretensions to the fisheries? Do we think national character so light a thing as to be willing to sacrifice the public faith to individual animosity?...

In this English cartoon the peace treaty of 1783 is attacked for supposedly leaving Loyalists at the mercy of the vengeful Americans.

[Britain had less to lose than America if the provisions of the treaty were not observed. Under the peace terms, Britain had recognized American independence, granted fishing rights, and agreed to surrender the western posts; America had given little in return.]

What equivalent do we give for this? Congress are to recommend the restoration of property to those who have adhered to her, and expressly engage that no future injury shall be done them on person liberty or property. This is the sole condition on our part where there is not an immediate reciprocity...and stands as the single equivalent for all the restitutions and concessions to be made by Great Britain. Will it be honest in us to violate this condition or will it be prudent to put it in competition with all the important matters to be performed on the other side? Will foreign nations be willing to undertake any thing with us or for us, when they find that the nature of our governments will allow no dependence to be placed upon our engagements?

I have omitted saying any thing of the impolicy of inducing by our severity a great number of useful citizens, whose situations do not make them a proper object of resentment to abandon the country to form settlements that will hereafter become our rivals animated with a hatred to us which will descend to their posterity. Nothing however can be more unwise than to contribute as we are doing to people the shores and wilderness of Nova-scotia, a colony which by its position will become a competitor with us among other things in that branch of commerce in which our navigation and navy will essentially depend. I mean the fisheries in which I have no doubt the state of New York will hereafter have a considerable share....

Those who consult only their passions might choose to construe what I say as too favourable to a set of men who have been the enemies of the public liberty; but those for whose esteem I am most concerned will acquit me of any personal considerations and will perceive that I only urge the cause of national honor, safety and advantage. We have assumed an independent station; we ought to feel and to act in a manner consistent with the dignity of that station.

I anxiously wish to see every prudent measure taken to prevent those combinations which will certainly disgrace us, if they do not involve us in other calamities. Whatever distinctions are judged necessary to be made in the case of those persons who have been in opposition to the common cause, let them be made by legal authority on a fair construction of the treaty, consistent with national faith and national honor.

Robert R. Livingston, circa 1804

After having returned to New York, Hamilton realized that persecution of the Tories could have far-reaching economic consequences for the state. Having passed through New York City on his way to Albany, he afterward sent this report to Robert R. Livingston, chancellor of New York State.

[Albany, August 13, 1783]
The spirit of emigration has greatly increased of late. Some violent papers sent into the city have determined many to depart, who hitherto have intended to remain. Many merchants of second class, characters of no political consequence, each of whom may carry away eight or ten thousand guineas have I am told lately applied for shipping to convey them away. Our state will feel for twenty years at least, the effects of the popular phrenzy.

While he waited for British troops to evacuate Manhattan, Hamilton shared his thoughts on America's political "peace establishment" with Washington and congratulated his former chief on the General's farewell address to the Army and the nation.

[Albany, September 30, 1783]

In a letter which I wrote to you several months ago I intimated that it might be in your power to contribute to the establishment of our Fœderal union upon a more solid basis. I have never since explained myself. At the time I was in hopes Congress might have been induced to take a decisive ground—to inform their constituents of the imperfections of the present system and of the impossibility of conducting the public affairs with honor to themselves and advantage to the community with powers so disproportioned to their responsibility; and having done this in a full and forcible manner, to adjourn the moment the definitive treaty was ratified. In retiring at the same juncture I wished you in a solemn manner to declare to the people your intended retreat from public concerns, your opinion of the present government and of the absolute necessity of a change.

Before I left Congress I dispaired of the first and your circular letter to the states had anticipated the last. I trust it will not be without effect though I am persuaded it would have had more combined with what I have mentioned. At all events, without compliment Sir, It will do you honor with the sensible and well meaning; and ultimately it is to be hoped with the people at large—when the present epidemic phrenzy has subsided.

A late-eighteenth-century view of Broadway and St. Paul's Chapel

While the "epidemic phrenzy" ran its course, Hamilton took the oaths required of a lawyer who wished to practice in New York courts and found a home for his family at 57 Wall Street in Manhattan. As soon as British forces left the city at the end of November, those Tories who had chosen to remain found themselves in need of legal advice. Hamilton's own disgust with public affairs and the demands of his growing practice led him to place this notice in the *New-York Packet.*

[New York, December 27, 1783]

I observe in Mr. Holt's paper [*The Independent New-York Gazette*] of this day, a nomination [for the state assembly] for the ensuing election, in which my name is included. I thank the authors of it for the honour they intended me; but being determined to decline public office, I think it proper to declare my determination, to avoid...distracting the votes of my fellow citizens.

Yet the interests of his clients did not allow Hamilton to ignore politics or public opinion. In January, 1784, he published his first *Letter from Phocion to the Considerate Citizens of New-York On the Politics of the Day*, which was concerned primarily with an "alien bill" passed in the state legislature in 1783. The bill, which would have threatened the civil rights of any man who had remained behind British lines during the Revolution, had been vetoed by the State Council of Revision but was about to be reconsidered by the legislature. Hamilton opened his pamphlet with an indictment of politicians who would "practise upon the passions of the people."

[New York, January 1–27, 1784]

It is...a common observation, that men, bent upon mischief, are more active in the pursuit of their object, than those who aim at doing good. Hence it is in the present moment, we see the most industrious efforts to violate, the constitution of this state, to trample upon the rights of the subject, and to chicane or infringe the most solemn obligations of treaty; while dispassionate and upright men almost totally neglect the means of counteracting these dangerous attempts. A sense of duty alone calls forth the observations which will be submitted to the good sense of the people in this paper, from one who has more inclination than leisure to serve them; and who has had too deep a share in the common exertions in this revolution, to be willing to see its fruits blasted by the violence of rash or unprincipled men, without at least protesting against their designs.

The persons alluded to, pretend to appeal to the spirit of Whiggism, while they endeavour to put in motion all the furious and dark passions of the human mind. The spirit of Whiggism, is generous, humane, beneficent and just. These men inculcate revenge, cruelty, persecutions, and perfidy. The spirit of Whiggism cherishes legal liberty, holds the rights of every individual sacred, condemns or punishes no man without regular trial and conviction of some crime declared by antecedent laws, reprobates equally the punishment of the citizen by arbitrary acts of legislature, as by the lawless combinations of unauthorised individuals: While these men are advocates for expelling a large number of their fellow-citizens unheard, untried; or if they

New York City in 1789 was confined to the lower tip of Manhattan and was bordered on the north by farms.

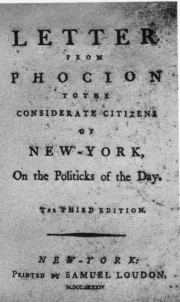

Title page from Hamilton's first Letter from Phocion, *dated 1784*

cannot effect this, are for disfranchising them, in the face of the constitution, without the judgment of their peers, and contrary to the law of the land....

[New Yorkers would endanger not only their own rights as citizens but also their economic future by expelling wealthy merchants with badly needed capital. There was, Hamilton insisted, nothing to fear from leaving former British sympathizers in peace.]

Viewing the subject in every possible light, there is not a single interest of the community but dictates moderation rather than violence. That honesty is still the best policy; that justice and moderation are the surest supports of every government, are maxims, which however they may be called trite, at all times true, though too seldom regarded, but rarely neglected with impunity. Were the people of America, with one voice, to ask, What shall we do to perpetuate our liberties and secure our happiness? The answer would be, "govern well" and you have nothing to fear either from internal disaffection or external hostility. Abuse not the power you possess, and you need never apprehend its diminution or loss. But if you make a wanton use of it, if you furnish another example, that despotism may debase the government of the many as well as the few, you like all others that have acted the same part, will experience that licentiousness is the fore-runner to slavery....

These sentiments are delivered to you in the frankness of conscious integrity, by one who *feels* that solicitude for the good of the community which the zealots, whose opinions he encounters profess, by one who pursues not as they do, the honour or emoluments of his country, by one who, though he has had, in the course of the Revolution, a very *confidential* share in the public councils, civil and military, and has as often, at least, met danger in the common cause as any of those who now assume to be the guardians of the public liberty, asks no other reward of his countrymen, than to be heard without prejudice for their own interest.

A month after this letter appeared, Hamilton gave his friend Gouverneur Morris a picture of New York politics and legal practice.

New York Feby. 21. 1784

Legislative folly has afforded so plentiful a harvest to us lawyers that we have scarcely a moment to spare from the substantial business of reaping. Today being sunday I have resolved to give an hour to friendship and to you. . . .

I ought . . . to give you an account of what we are doing here; but I will in the lump tell you that we are doing those things which we ought not to do, and leaving undone those things which we ought to do. Instead of wholesome regulations for the improvement of our polity and commerce; we are labouring to contrive methods to mortify and punish tories and to explain away treaties.

Let us both erect a temple to time; only regretting that we shall not command a longer portion of it to see what will be the event of the American drama.

Hamilton's first *Letter from Phocion* did not go unchallenged. A reply from "Mentor" appeared in short order, and a second *Letter from Phocion* was necessary to answer "Mentor's" charges and to prepare public opinion for the stand Hamilton would take in the New York courts as the defense attorney for Joshua Waddington, a New Yorker who was being sued under the state's Trespass Act. Hamilton pointed out that more than the fate of a few Tories, more than the honor of the state or even of the nation, were involved.

[New York, April, 1784]

Those, who are at present entrusted with power, in all these infant republics, hold the most sacred deposit that ever was confided to human hands. 'Tis with governments as with individuals, first impressions and early habits give a lasting bias to the temper and character. Our governments hitherto have no habits. How important to the happiness not of America alone, but of mankind, that they should acquire good ones. . . .

The world has its eye upon America. The noble struggle we have made in the cause of liberty, has occasioned a kind of revolution in human sentiment. The influence of our example has penetrated the gloomy regions of despotism, and has pointed the way to inquiries, which may shake it to its deepest foundations. Men begin to ask every where, who is this tyrant, that dares to build his greatness on our misery and degradation? What commission has he to sacrifice millions to the wanton appetites of himself and the few minions that surround his throne? . . .

If the consequences prove, that we really have asserted the cause of human happiness, what may not be expected from so illustrious an example? In a greater or less degree, the world will bless and imitate!

But if experience, in this instance, verifies the lesson long taught by the enemies of liberty; that the bulk of mankind are not fit to govern themselves, that they must have a master, and were only made for the rein and the spur: We shall then see the final triumph of despotism over liberty. . . . With the greatest advantages for promoting it, that ever a people had, we shall have betrayed the cause of human nature.

Let those in whose hands it is placed, pause for a moment, and contemplate with an eye of reverence, the vast trust committed to them. Let them retire into their own bosoms and examine the motives which there prevail. Let them ask themselves this solemn question —Is the sacrifice of a few mistaken, or criminal individuals, an object worthy of the shifts to which we are reduced to evade the constitution and the national engagements? Then let them review the arguments that have been offered . . . and if they even doubt the propriety of the measures, they may be about to adopt, let them remember, that in a doubtful case, the constitution ought never to be hazarded, without extreme necessity.

New York Attorney General Egbert Benson, a Hamilton opponent in the case of Rutgers v. Waddington

Before the *Second Letter from Phocion* appeared, Hamilton had been retained by Joshua Waddington, the defendant in a suit brought by Mrs. Elizabeth Rutgers under the Trespass Act. Mrs. Rutgers, the operator of a brewery, had fled New York City in 1776. During the occupation, British civil authorities, and later the military, had given permission to two English merchants to operate the brewery, and Mrs. Rutgers was now seeking back rent and damages of eight thousand pounds from Waddington, who was an agent for the merchants. In his plea on Waddington's behalf, Hamilton argued that the Trespass Act violated the "law of nations" by not allowing citizens to plead military orders as a defense for actions that might otherwise have been illegal. Using traditional legal phrases, he also implied that the act was void because it violated the Treaty of Paris.

[April 21, 1784]

Joshua Waddington further saith, that the... action... against him ought not to have and maintain; because he saith that after the passing the act of the Legislature of this state... a certain definitive treaty of peace between the King of Great Britain and... the United States of America... was entered into made and concluded...; which said definitive treaty of peace hath been since ... by the said United States of America in Congress... approved ratified and confirmed, and was afterwards... announced published and notified to all the good Citizens of the said United States... the said proclamation requiring and enjoining all bodies of Magistracy, Legislative executive and judiciary, all persons bearing office civil and military of whatever rank... and all... the good Citizens of the said States of every vocation and condition, that reverencing those stipulations entered into on their behalf under the authority of that foederal bond by which their existence as an independent people is bound up together and is known and acknowleged by the nations of the world and with that good faith which is every mans surest guide— ... they should carry into effect the said definitive Articles and every clause and sentence thereof strictly and completely... in virtue of which said definitive treaty, all right claim pretension and demand whatsoever which either of the said contracting parties and the Subjects and Citizens of either of the said contracting parties might otherwise have had to any compensation, recompence, retribution or indemnity whatsoever; for or by reason of any injury or damage... which either of the said contracting parties might have done or caused to be done to the other... and the Subjects and Citizens of the other... in consequence of or in any wise relating to the war... virtually and effectually relinquished renounced and released to each other to all intents constructions and purposes whatsoever.

A check, signed by Aaron Burr, drawn on the Bank of New York

R*utgers* v. *Waddington* was at best a qualified success for Hamilton. The New York Mayor's Court, while avoiding ruling on the legality of the Trespass Act, held that the legislature had not intended to overrule the "law of nations," since nothing to that effect was specifically stated in the act. The court also ruled that Mrs. Rutgers was entitled to collect rent only for the period when the merchants held her property under the orders of a civilian and not for the years when they were licensed by British military authorities.

The Trespass and Confiscation acts were not Hamilton's only concerns in 1784. In the preceding summer, his wife's brother-in-law, John Barker Church, had sailed for Europe, leaving Hamilton in charge of his interests in New York. Church and his partner, Jeremiah Wadsworth, hoped to found a commercial bank in Manhattan, but Robert R. Livingston, the state chancellor, sponsored a rival scheme for a bank whose capital would be largely in pledges of land. Hamilton set about mobilizing support for a "money bank," and the Bank of New York was organized on March 15. Three weeks later, Hamilton, who had originally favored competition in banking, conveyed his modified views on the subject in a letter to Gouverneur Morris.

[New York, April 7, 1784]

...you will believe me when I tell you, that on more deliberate consideration, I was led to view the competition in a different light from that in which it at first struck me. I had no doubt that it was against the interests of the proprietors; but on a superficial view I perceived benefits to the community which on a more close inspection I found were not real.

You well call our proceedings here *strange doings*; if some folks were paid to counteract the prosperity of the state, they could not take more effectual measures than they do. But it is in vain to attempt to kick against the Pricks.

Discrimination bills—Partial taxes—schemes to engross public property in the hands of those who have present power—to banish the real wealth of the state and substitute paper bubbles are the only dishes that suit the public palate at this time.

Page from New York Mayor's Court docket, 1784, signed by Hamilton

For the remainder of the year, Hamilton was engrossed in the details of establishing the Bank of New York and handling his growing law practice. Meanwhile, the pleasures of life in New York were increased when John Jay and his family returned from Europe in the summer. Jay, who became Secretary for Foreign Affairs, joined Hamilton in leading a reform movement that both had been advocating for several years—the end of slavery. Early in February, 1785, they met with other antislavery New Yorkers to form the Society for Promoting the Manumission of Slaves. The minutes of that meeting provide a record of some of Hamilton's activities.

[New York, February 4, 1785]

Ordered—That Colonel Hamilton, Colonel [Robert] Troup and Mr. [White] Matlack be a Committee to Report

"What the unhappy Children of Africa endure"—an illustration from an emancipation broadside of 1807

a Line of Conduct to be recommended to the Members of the Society in relation to any Slaves possessed by them; and also to prepare a Recommendation to all such Persons as have manumitted or shall Manumit Slaves to transmit their names and the names and Ages of the Slaves manumitted; in Order that the same may be Registered and the Society be the better Enabled to detect Attempts to deprive such Manumitted Persons of their Liberty.

Hamilton's family responsibilities, meantime, were increasing. A baby girl, Angelica, had been added to the family, and Betsey Schuyler Hamilton looked after her children while her husband traveled the "circuit" of New York courts. A letter written in mid-March shows that Hamilton found his "Angel" to be a competent businesswoman as well as a loving wife.

> [West Chester, New York, March 17, 1785]
> I have just written to you My beloved by the person who will probably be the bearer of this. Col Burr just tells me, that the house we live in is offered for sale at £2100. I am to request you to agree for the purchase for me, if at that price. If you cannot do better, you may engage that the whole shall be paid in three months; but I could wish to pay half in a short time and the other half in a year. Adieu my Angel
>
> A HAMILTON

In the spring of 1785, Hamilton again found his name being put forward for public office. Again he refused to run, but when the state legislature defeated a petition for a charter of incorporation for the Bank of New York, he set out to persuade other "men of respectability" to enter politics. Toward the end of April he broached the subject to Robert Livingston, the lord of the Manor of Livingston.

> [April 25, 1785]
> ...the situation of the state at this time is so critical that it is become a serious object of attention to those who are concerned for the *security of property* or the prosperity of government, to endeavour to put men in the Legislature whose principles are not of the *levelling kind*. The spirit of the present Legislature is truly alarming, and appears evidently directed to the confusion of all property and principle. The truth is that the state

One of Hamilton's pleas before the
New York Supreme Court, July, 1785

is now governed by a couple of New England adventurers.... A number of attempts have been made by this junto to subvert the constitution and destroy the rights of private property.... All men of respectability, in the city, of whatever party, who have been witnesses of the despotism and iniquity of the Legislature, are convinced, that the principal people in the community must for their own defence, unite to overset the party I have alluded to. I wish you to be persuaded Sir, that I would not take the liberty to trouble you with these remarks with a view to serving any particular turn; but, from a thorough conviction, that the safety of all those who have any thing to lose calls upon them to take care that the power of government is intrusted to proper hands. Much depends on the ensuing election. You Sir have much in your power; and I have no doubt you will have heared from other quarters and from your immediate connections, a like account of public affairs to that which I have now given.

In the summer and early fall of 1785, Hamilton devoted much of his time to research on a commission that was to settle a boundary dispute between New York and Massachusetts. Among his business letters, receipts, and legal documents from this period, there is one poignant reminder of Hamilton's boyhood, of the life he had left behind in the West Indies. In June, Hamilton received a letter from his older brother James, a carpenter. James's letter has been lost, but Alexander's reply gives a good idea of James's circumstances and of Alexander's wish to help his brother and reunite his family.

New York, June 22, 1785.

The situation you describe yourself to be in gives me much pain, and nothing will make me happier than, as far as may be in my power, to contribute to your relief. I will cheerfully pay your draft upon me for fifty pounds sterling, whenever it shall appear. I wish it was in my power to desire you to enlarge the sum; but though my future prospects are of the most flattering kind my present engagements would render it inconvenient to me to advance you a larger sum. My affection for you, however, will not permit me to be inattentive to your welfare, and I hope time will prove to you that I feel all the sentiment of a brother. Let me only request of you to exert your industry for a year or two more where

Angelica Schuyler Church

Cornelia Schuyler

you are, and at the end of that time I promise myself to be able to invite you to a more comfortable settlement in this Country. Allow me only to give you one caution, which is to avoid if possible getting in debt. Are you *married* or *single*? If the *latter*, it is my wish for many reasons it may be agreeable to you to continue in that state.

But what has become of our dear father? It is an age since I have heared from him or of him, though I have written him several letters. Perhaps, alas! he is no more, and I shall not have the pleasing opportunity of contributing to render the close of his life more happy than the progress of it. My heart bleeds at the recollection of his misfortunes and embarrassments. Sometimes I flatter myself his brothers have extended their support to him, and that he now enjoys tranquillity and ease. At other times I fear he is suffering in indigence. I entreat you, if you can, to relieve me from my doubts, and let me know how or where he is, if alive, if dead, how and where he died. Should he be alive inform him of my inquiries, beg him to write to me, and tell him how ready I shall be to devote myself and all I have to his accommodation and happiness.

I do not advise your coming to this country at present, for the war has also put things out of order here, and people in your business find a subsistence difficult enough. My object will be, by-and-by, to get you settled on a farm.

Believe me always your affectionate friend and brother,

ALEX. HAMILTON.

Alexander Hamilton never saw his brother again, for James Hamilton died the following year. Fortunately, Hamilton had found a family that he adopted as completely as any man could—the Schuylers. His wife's parents, brothers, and sisters had accepted him as one of their own, and Hamilton repaid their affection in full. When he learned that his sister-in-law, Angelica Schuyler Church, and her husband might remain in Europe, Hamilton pleaded with his "Dear Sister" to reconsider.

[New York, August 3, 1785]
You have I fear taken a final leave of America and of those that love you here. I saw you depart from Philadelphia with peculiar uneasiness, as if foreboding you

were not to return. My apprehensions are confirmed and unless I see you in Europe I expect not to see you again.

This is the impression we all have; judge the bitterness it gives to those who love you with the *love of nature* and to me who feel an attachment for you not less lively.

I confess for my own part I see one great source of happiness snatched away. My affection for Church and yourself made me anticipate much enjoyment in your friendship and neighbourhood. But an ocean is now to separate us.

Let me entreat you both not precipitately to wed yourselves to a soil less propitious to you than will be that of America: You will not indeed want friends wherever you are on two accounts: One is You will have no need of them: another is that You have both too many qualities to engage friend ship. But go where you will you will find no *such* friends as those you have left behind.

In the fall of 1785, local "prejudices" and party politics again began to interrupt Hamilton's private pursuits. On September 13, the Pennsylvania legislature, dominated by the "Constitutionalist" party, repealed the charter of the Bank of North America. The bank still held a charter from Congress—but not from the state in which it was located. Since Hamilton's wife's brother-in-law John Barker Church and Church's associate Jeremiah Wadsworth were large stockholders in this bank, the battles between Pennsylvania's Constitutionalists and Republicans became a pressing concern for Hamilton. Toward the end of October he wrote urgently to Wadsworth in Hartford, Connecticut.

[New York, October 29, 1785]

What do you intend to do or what would you advise to be done for Mr Church? To sell unless at a great disadvantage is not practicable. To leave *so considerable a sum* in a Company of this kind not incorporated is too dangerous. To force it out of their hands is an uphill business. In this choice of difficulties I will submit to you what occurs to me.

It is believed the Republican party has prevailed at the last election, not in so decisive a manner however as to insure a decisive influence; but sufficiently in all probability to effect a revival of the act of Incorporation.

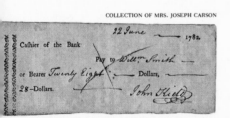

One of the earliest existing checks drawn on the Bank of North America

151

Should this happen, It will in some degree restore the credit of stock and make it easier to part with it, without any considerable loss.

I should think therefore it would be prudent to wait the result of the next meeting of their Legislature; if the Charter is not then revived, I should be of opinion to insist that measures may be taken to decide the Question whether the bank still remains an incorporated body by virtue of the original act of Congress or not.... The mode of deciding it will be easy. It will be to get some person to refuse to pay a note to the bank, and to have an action instituted against him in behalf of the bank in their corporate capacity. If the Courts allow this action to be maintained it must be on the principle that the Bank still subsists a corporation in Pensylvania.

If the decision is in favour of the corporate existence of the bank, the proprietors will then know in what situation they are and may either continue such with greater safety or part with their interest with less disadvantage. If it is decided that the bank does not continue a corporation, you can then insist on your money being returned to you and may compel its being done. It seems to me essential you should ascertain upon what footing you stand.

Jeremiah Wadsworth

Wadsworth replied immediately, reporting that he had already had doubts about the Bank of North America and had made an unsuccessful attempt to force the bank to return the funds he had invested. Hamilton accordingly prepared a letter of instructions to Wadsworth, who was to act as the agent for John Church and four other stockholders in the bank. At a meeting of the shareholders on January 9, 1786, Wadsworth presented the letter as a summary of his position.

[New York, January 3, 1786]

Those who subscribed to the Bank of North America on the faith of the Pensylvania Charter might with great reason urge that so material a change in its situation is, at all events, with respect to them, a dissolution of the contract upon which their subscriptions were made; and that they have a right to reclaim their property. But not being disposed to agitate any questions injurious to the Institution, we are content to wave this right, so long as there remains any prospect of the bank being continued with safety and advantage. This prospect

The Critical Period of American History BY JOHN FISKE

This set of scales for weighing coins was used by a Connecticut town clerk during the late eighteeenth century.

however we deem inseparable from its existence as a corporation; and if this cannot be maintained all hopes of security or utility in our apprehension fail.

Nothing will give us greater pleasure than to find that the Bank of North America has a solid foundation in the Charter of the United States; and that it will on experiment be considered in this light by the laws of that state in which from its position its operations would be carried on; but it appears to us essential that the experiment should be made without delay, in order that it may be ascertained in what light it will be considered by those laws. If these should pronounce that it is no corporation, no prudent alternative is left but to remove it to another state, where it will be protected by the laws, or to leave all those who wish to do it at liberty to withdraw their shares.

While on the one hand public as well as private considerations concur to restrain us from advising any measures incompatible with the Interest of the bank; on the other hand we cannot help feeling great anxiety to know what our *true* situation is; and to extricate ourselves from *one* (if such *it* is) in which we might hazard much more than we intended.

Slowly but surely, Hamilton's interest in public affairs was being revived. In early 1786, an old cause — the impost — called Hamilton to action. The import duty recommended by Congress in April, 1783, had been approved by every state but Georgia and New York. Georgia was on the verge of granting its approval, but New York, which enjoyed a sizable revenue from state taxes on imports, was reluctant to share this source of wealth with the Federal treasury. Hamilton drafted a petition to the state legislature advocating acceptance of the tax in the spring session.

[New York, January–March, 1786]

The Petition of the Subscribers Inhabitants of the City of New York respectfully sheweth...

That the anxiety which Your Petitioners have all along felt from motives of a more general nature is at the present junction increased by this particular consideration that the State of New York now stands almost alone, in a non compliance with a measure in which the sentiments and wishes of the Union at large appear to unite and by a further delay may render itself responsible for consequences too serious not to affect every considerate man.

That in the opinion of Your Memorialists all the considerations important to a state—all the motives of public honor faith reputation interest and safety conspire to urge a compliance with these resolutions.

That Government without revenue cannot subsist. That the mode provided in the Confederation for supplying the treasury of the United States has in experiment been found inadequate.

That the system proposed will in all probability prove much more efficacious, and is in other respects as unexceptionable as the various circumstances and interests of these states will permit.

That any objection to it as a measure not warranted by the confederation is refuted by the thirteenth article which provides that alterations may be made if agreed to by Congress and confirmed by the Legislatures of each State....

That as to danger in vesting the United States with these funds, Your Memorialists consider their interests and liberties as not less safe in the hands of their fellow citizens delegated to represent them for one year in Congress than in the hands of their fellow citizens delegated to represent them for one year or four years in the Senate and Assembly of this state.

That Government implies trust; and every government must be trusted so far as is necessary to enable it to attain the ends for which it is instituted; without which insult and oppression from abroad confusion and convulsion at home.

To the south, meanwhile, there were promising signs for nationalists. James Madison and George Washington had successfully sponsored arbitration that ended a dispute between Virginia and Maryland over navigation rights on the Potomac River. This in turn led to a call from the Virginia assembly for a convention to "take into consideration the trade of the states" and "seek a uniform system in their commercial regulations." By now Hamilton was ready once again to play an active role in the nationalist cause, as was evident in a letter he sent to Nathaniel Hazard. Hazard, a New York ironmonger, had asked Hamilton's help in supporting a petition addressed to the legislature on behalf of New Yorkers who were indebted to British merchants. Hamilton's reply was "politic" in more than one respect.

The State House at Annapolis, site of the Annapolis Convention, 1786

[New York, April 24, 1786]

I would not be understood to declare any opinion concerning the principles of the Bill, with which I am not sufficiently acquainted to form a decided opinion. I have merely made your letter the occasion of Introducing the subject to General Schuyler; whose sentiments are as favorable to your wishes as you could desire.

I make this observation from that spirit of candour which I hope will always direct my conduct. I am aware that I have been represented as an enemy to the wishes of what you call your corps. If by this has been meant that I do not feel as much as any man, not immediately interested, for the distresses of those merchants who have been in a great measure the victims of the revolution, the supposition does not do Justice either to my head or my heart. But if it means that I have always viewed the mode of relieving them as a matter of peculiar delicacy and difficulty it is well founded.

I should have thought it unnecessary to enter into this explanation, were it not that I am held up as a candidate at the ensuing Election; and I would not wish that the step I have taken in respect to your letter should be considered as implying more than it does: For I woud never wish to conciliate at the expence of candour. On the other hand, I confide in your liberality not to infer more than I intend from the explanation I have given.

Six days later, Hamilton was elected to the assembly from New York County. In May, when the legislature agreed to send commissioners to the convention, which was to be held in September at Annapolis, Maryland, Hamilton was among those elected to the delegation. At about this same time he also had the satisfaction of celebrating the birth of his third child, Alexander, Jr. Leaving his growing family at the end of the summer, Hamilton traveled to Annapolis, and shortly after reaching his destination he wrote to his wife to assure her of his safe arrival.

[Annapolis, September 8, 1786]

I was not very well on the first part of the journey; but my health has been improved by travelling and is now as good as I could wish. Happy, however I cannot be, absent from you and my darling little ones. I feel that nothing can ever compensate for the loss of the enjoyments I leave at home, or can ever put my heart at tolerable ease. In the bosom of my family alone must my happiness be sought, and in that of my Betsey is every thing that is charming to me. Would to heaven I were there! Does not your heart re-echo the wish?

In reality my attachments to home disqualify me for either business or pleasure abroad; and the prospect of a detention here for Eight or ten days perhaps a fortnight fills me with an anxiety which will best be conceived by my Betseys own impatience.

I am straitened for time & must conclude.... Kiss my little ones a thousand times for me.... Think of me with as much tenderness as I do of you and we cannot fail to be always happy[.]

Events proved that Hamilton was by no means so "disqualified" for public service by his "attachments to home" as he expected to be. On the surface, the Annapolis Convention seemed a poor starting place for reform of the American Government. Only five states were represented, and the delegates met for only four days. But the fact that this convention could do nothing constructive in the area of commercial regulation made it possible for some of the commissioners to suggest another convention where there would be a fuller representation of the states and where a broader range of topics might be discussed. The delegates from New Jersey had been instructed to discuss "other important matters" as well as trade, and Hamilton seized on this idea in drafting the address issued by the convention at the close of its sessions.

[Annapolis, September 14, 1786]
Your Commissioners cannot forbear to indulge an expression of their earnest and unanimous wish, that speedy measures may be taken, to effect a general meeting, of the States, in a future Convention, for the same and such other purposes, as the situation of public affairs, may be found to require....

In this persuasion your Commissioners submit an opinion, that the Idea of extending the powers of their Deputies, to other objects, than those of Commerce,... will deserve to be incorporated into that of a future Convention....

That there are important defects in the system of the Fœderal Government is acknowledged by the Acts of all those States, which have concurred in the present Meeting; That the defects, upon a closer examination, may be found greater and more numerous, than even these acts imply, is at least so far probable...as may

The insignia of the Society of the Cincinnati, as it appeared on an invitation to a Society banquet

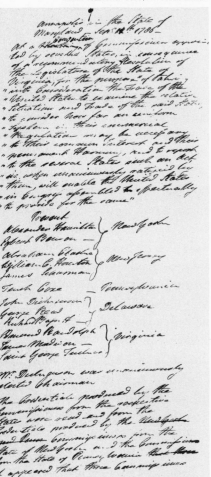

The minutes of the meeting of the Annapolis Convention of September 11, 1786, showing those present to include Hamilton and James Madison

reasonably be supposed to merit a deliberate and candid discussion, in some mode, which will unite the Sentiments and Councils of all the States. In the choice of the mode your Commissioners are of opinion, that a Convention of Deputies from the different States, for the special and sole purpose of entering into this investigation, and digesting a plan for supplying such defects as may be discovered to exist, will be entitled to a preference....

Your Commissioners, with the most respectful deference, beg leave to suggest their unanimous conviction, that it may essentially tend to advance the interests of the union, if the States, by whom they have been respectively delegated, would themselves concur, and use their endeavours to procure the concurrence of the other States, in the appointment of Commissioners, to meet at Philadelphia on the second Monday in May next, to take into consideration the situation of the United States, to devise such further provisions as shall appear to them necessary to render the constitution of the Fœderal Government adequate to the exigencies of the Union; and to report such an Act for that purpose to the United States in Congress Assembled, as when agreed to, by them, and afterwards confirmed by the Legislatures of every State will effectually provide for the same.

Though your Commissioners could not with propriety address these observations and sentiments to any but the States they have the honor to Represent, they have nevertheless concluded from motives of respect, to transmit Copies of this report to the United States in Congress assembled, and to the executives of the other States.

After Hamilton returned to New York to await the reconvening of the state legislature in January, 1787, an opportunity arose for him to advance the nationalist cause. The Society of the Cincinnati, a fraternal organization of Revolutionary officers, had been attacked for its supposedly aristocratic pretensions, and the national society had suggested reforms in the bylaws. As a member of the committee named by the New York chapter to correspond with other state societies, Hamilton drafted comments on some of the proposed alterations in the national charter. One such proposal called for the deletion of a clause that stated that one of the group's fundamental principles was "to promote and cherish between the respective States that Union and national honor so essentially necessary, to their Happiness and the future dignity of the American empire." Hamilton argued vigorously that the passage should be retained.

[New York, November, 1786]

We flatter ourselves, we speak the sense of the Society of which we are members, as well as our own, in declaring, that we reverence the sentiment contained in that clause, too much to be willing to see it expunged. Nor can we believe that its continuance will on reflection, give umbrage to any whose views are not unfriendly to those principles which form the Basis of the Union and the only sure foundation of the tranquility and happiness of this Country. To such men it can never appear criminal, that a class of citizens who have had so conspicuous an Agency in the American Revolution as those who compose the Society of the Cincinnati should pledge themselves to each other, in a voluntary association, to support, by all means consistent with the laws, That noble Fabric of United Independence, which at so much hazard, and with so many sacrifices they have contributed to erect; a Fabric on the Solidity and duration of which the value of all they have done must depend! And America can never have cause to condemn, an Institution, calculated to give energy and extent to a sentiment, favorable to the preservation of that Union, by which she established her liberties, and to which she must owe her future peace, respectability and prosperity. Experience, we doubt not, will teach her, that the members of the Cincinnati, always actuated by the same virtuous and generous motives, which have hitherto directed their conduct, will pride themselves in being, thro every vicissitude of her future fate, the steady and faithful supporters of her Liberty, her Laws and her Government.

A 1787 deed of settlement of the Mutual Assurance Company, of which Hamilton was an early director

Hamilton had had almost three and a half years of retirement from public life in which to study state and national problems. Now, with the New York Assembly about to reconvene, he faced a test of his ability to adapt to the realities of American politics. If he proved himself in that legislature, he could go on to serve America, "her Liberty, her Laws and her Government," at the coming Constitutional Convention in Philadelphia, where he would need all his skills as a forceful courtroom lawyer to win his case for a strong national government.

Chapter 6

Prelude to Nationhood

When Alexander Hamilton took his seat in the New York Assembly in January, 1787, he was well aware that Governor George Clinton, the leader of the forces that had fought Continental measures after the war, would oppose any future attempt to surrender state power to a national government. A capable and conscientious man, Clinton had been a popular and effective governor since 1777. First and always a state leader rather than a national politician, he cited constitutional reasons for his opposition to a national impost; but clearly, a more important factor was his reluctance to see nationwide taxes deprive the state of its own highly profitable levies.

Conflict between Hamilton and Clinton was inevitable, for the points Hamilton was determined to win in the legislature were diametrically opposed to the views held by the governor. Hamilton hoped, first of all, that the legislature would reconsider the list of qualifications it had attached to its approval of the impost in the spring of 1786—qualifications that could not be accepted by other states. He also intended to do all he could to modify the laws concerning Loyalists. Most important, Hamilton intended to use every opportunity to convince the legislature that the crisis in national affairs demanded that New York participate in the Philadelphia Convention. To achieve his objectives, he shrewdly pictured Clinton as a man who had enjoyed power so long that he was no longer willing to share it, as a man who might even be willing to infringe on the rights of the citizens of his state. In contrast, Hamilton represented himself as the defender of the state constitution, the champion of popular rights. Although his oratory did not persuade the legislature to vote with him in every case, he did win the respect of the legislators and was named a delegate to the convention.

The legislative session opened on January 13, 1787, with the governor's annual message, in which Clinton summarized his reasons for having ignored a congressional request that the legislature be called into special session to reconsider its position on the impost. Hamilton, a member of the committee that was to prepare the assembly's reply, submitted a draft that contained no reference to the governor's action. Clinton's supporters demanded that the assembly express its approval of Clinton's decision. The battle was on. In his first speech in this debate, Hamilton dwelled on the governor's contention that a special session would have impaired "the right of free deliberation on matters not stipulated by the [Articles of] Confederation."

[New York, January 19, 1787]

In particular I think it must strike us all, that there is something singularly forced in intimating, that an application of Congress to the governor of the state to convene a new legislature to consider a very important national subject, has any thing in it dangerous to the freedom of our deliberations. I flatter myself we should all have felt ourselves, as much at liberty to have pursued our sentiments, if we had met upon an extraordinary call, as we now do when met according to our own appointment.

There yet remains an important light, in which the subject merits consideration, I mean as it respects the executive authority of the state itself. By deciding that the application of Congress upon which the debate turns was not such an extraordinary occasion as left the governor at liberty to call the legislature, we may form a precedent of a very dangerous tendency; we may impose a sense on the constitution very different from the true meaning of it—and may fetter the present, or a future executive with very inconvenient restraints. A few more such precedents may tie up the hands of a governor in such a manner, as would either oblige him to act at an extreme peril or to omit acting when public exigencies required it. The mere sense of one governor would be no precedent for his successor, but that sense approved by both houses of the legislature would become a rule of conduct. . . .

[Hamilton then turned to the argument that there was a "danger" in implying that Congress could "compel" state legislatures to convene.]

Admitting in the fullest extent that it would be dangerous to allow to Congress the power of requiring the legislature to be convened at pleasure, yet no injury nor inconvenience can result from supposing the call of the United States on a matter by them deemed of importance to be an occasion sufficiently extraordinary to *authorise*,

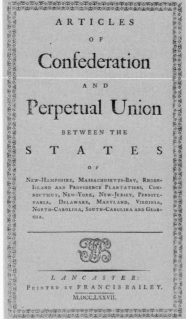

ARTICLES

OF

Confederation

AND

Perpetual Union

BETWEEN THE

STATES

OF

NEW-HAMPSHIRE, MASSACHUSETTS-BAY, RHODE-ISLAND AND PROVIDENCE PLANTATIONS, CONNECTICUT, NEW-YORK, NEW-JERSEY, PENNSYLVANIA, DELAWARE, MARYLAND, VIRGINIA, NORTH-CAROLINA, SOUTH-CAROLINA AND GEORGIA.

LANCASTER:
PRINTED BY FRANCIS BAILEY.
M,DCC,LXXVII.

Title page of the Articles of Confederation, published in 1777

160

not to *oblige* the governor to comply with it.

I cannot forbear remarking, that it is a common artifice to endeavour to insinuate a resemblance between the king under the former government, and Congress; though no two things can be more unlike each other. Nothing can be more dissimilar than a monarch, permanent, hereditary, the source of honor and emolument; and a republican body composed of a number of individuals appointed annu[a]lly, liable to be recalled within the year, and subject to a continual rotation, which with few exceptions, is the fountain neither of honor nor emolument. If we will exercise our judgments we shall plainly see that no such resemblance exists, and that all inferences deducted from the comparison must be false.

Upon every occasion, however foreign such observations may be, we hear a loud cry raised about the danger of intrusting power to Congress, we are told it is dangerous to trust power any where; that *power* is liable to *abuse* with a variety of trite maxims of the same kind. . . . To these we might oppose other propositions equally true and equally indefinite. It might be said that too little power is as dangerous as too much, that it leads to anarchy, and from anarchy to despotism. But the question still recurs, what is this *too much or too little?* where is the measure or standard to ascertain the happy mean?

Powers must be granted, or civil Society cannot exist; the possibility of abuse is no argument against the *thing;* this possibility is incident to every species of power however placed or modified.

Governor George Clinton

Samuel Jones of Queens County led the forces demanding praise for Clinton's stand. In his reply to Hamilton's speech, Jones argued that there would be no constitutional issue in the assembly's expressing its approval, and he elaborated on the perils of letting Congress interfere in local government. When Jones concluded, Hamilton rose to make his second speech of the day. After answering the points Jones had raised, Hamilton introduced a new issue—a particularly significant one in view of the call for a national convention.

[New York, January 19, 1787]

Sir, are we not to respect federal decisions; are we on the contrary to take every opportunity of holding up their resolutions and requests in a contemptible and insignificant light, and tell the world, their calls, their requests are nothing to us, that we are bound by none of their measures; do not let us add to their embarrassment, for it is but a slender tie that at present holds us, you see alas what contempt we are falling into since the peace; you see to what our commerce is exposed to on every side. You see us the laughing stock, the sport of foreign nations, and what may this lead to? I dread Sir, to think. Little will it avail then to say, we could not attend to your wise and earnest requests without inconvenience; little will it avail to say it would have hurt individual interest to have left our farms. These things are trifling when compared to bringing the Councils and powers of the Union into universal contempt, by saying their call was unimportant.... See, gentlemen, before you feel what may be your situation hereafter. There is more involved in this measure than what presents itself to your view.

The first round of legislative battle went to Clinton when the assembly voted to include a brief commendation in its reply to the governor's message. Hamilton had more success in debates on a bill regulating state elections. A provision was introduced barring any "person receiving a pension from, or holding any office or place under" the national government from holding a seat in the state legislature. In a speech, reported in the *Daily Advertiser,* Hamilton shrewdly presented himself as a defender of the state constitution.

[New York, January 27, 1787]

It is impossible to suppose that the Convention who framed the constitution were inattentive to this point. It is a matter of too much importance not to have been well considered, they have fixed the qualification of electors with precision; they have defined those of Senator and Governor; but they have been silent as to the qualifications of Members of Assembly. It may be said that, being silent, they have left the matter to the discretion of the legislature. But is not the language of the framers of the constitution rather this?—we will fix the qualifications of electors—we will take care that persons absolutely indigent shall be excluded—we will provide that the right of voting shall be on a broad and secure basis—and we will trust to the discretion of the electors themselves the choice of those who are to represent them in assembly. Every qualification implies a disqualification: The persons who do not possess the qualification required become ineligible. Is not this to restrain the freedom of choice allowed by the constitution to the body of electors? . . .

By the constitution every citizen is eligible to a seat in the Assembly. If we say certain descriptions of persons shall not be so eligible, what is this but to deprive all those who fall within that description of an essential right allowed them by the constitution? . . .

[If the legislature of 1787 broke faith with the constitution, Hamilton charged, future legislatures could carry the principle further. Then he turned to specific problems that the bill could cause.]

I have hitherto confined my self to the general principle of the clause. There are however particular objections, one just occurs to me—there are officers who have been wounded in the service, and who now have pensions under the United States as the price of their blood; would it be just, would it not be cruel on this account to exclude men from a share in the administration of that government which they have at every hazard contributed to establish? . . .

If the committee however should resolve to adopt it; for the sake of consistency, they must carry it one step further—they must say that no member of Congress shall hold a seat. For surely if it be dangerous that the servants of Congress should have a seat in this house, it is more dangerous that the members themselves should be allowed this privilege.

But I would not be understood to advocate this extention of the clause. I am against the whole business. I am for adhering strictly to the present provisions of the constitution, I repeat it if we once break the ground of innovation, we may open a door to mischiefs what we neither know nor think of.

Hamilton carried his point; the clause on Continental pensioners and officeholders was deleted. A day later, he condemned another article in the elections bill, which would have required inspectors to "take aside" illiterate voters "and examine them" concerning their choices on the ballot. This time, Hamilton managed to emerge as the champion of the rights of the uneducated masses.

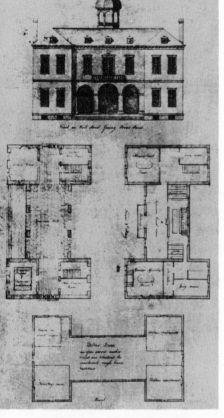

The façade and floor plans of New York's old City Hall on Wall Street, where the state assembly met in 1787

[New York, January 30, 1787]

It was very justly remarked . . . that the unlettered person from his want of knowing personally the candidates will not when taken aside recollect the names even of them, or at least but a few; in this case the inspector not only may, but must suggest the names to him otherwise how can he vote? What then is the consequence? Certainly if he is a man connected with party, he will vote for his friend, for notwithstanding the inspector may be an honest man, and bound by an oath on this occasion, yet, we know how easy it is for people to interpret such oaths to accommodate themselves, especially when they think they are rendering service to their country, they find a thousand ingenious contrivances, a thousand subterfuges to reconcile it to their preferences.

But . . . it not only is dangerous but it is totally contrary to the very genius and intention of balloting; which means that a man's vote should be secret and known but to himself—yet you not only permit him but even oblige him to discover his vote. . . . this clause is a violation of the right we wish to give ourselves of voting concealed, and it deprives the unlettered person of what his fellow citizen who has it in his power to read, has secured to him. I would wish these persons might be left to themselves, for there would be then less danger than when the influence was regular.

On February 9, an impost bill was reintroduced in the assembly. Fighting for the bill's unconditional acceptance, Hamilton repeated the arguments he had perfected over four years to show that the impost would not infringe on state rights or state constitutions. In the end, he turned to an aspect of the situation that was closest to his heart.

[New York, February 15, 1787]

Let us ask ourselves what will be the consequence of rejecting the bill; what will be the situation of our national affairs if they are left much longer to float in the chaos in which they are now involved.

Can our national character be preserved without paying our debts. Can the union subsist without revenue. Have we realized the consequences which would attend its dissolution.

If these states are not united under a federal government, they will infalliably have wars with each other;

and their divisions will subject them to all the mischiefs of foreign influence and intrigue. The human passions will never want objects of hospitality. The western territory is an obvious and fruitful source of contest. Let us also cast our eye upon the mass of this state, intersected from one extremity to the other by a large navigable river. In the event of a rupture with them, what is to hinder our metropolis from becoming a prey to our neighbours? Is it even supposeable that they would suffer it to remain the nursery of wealth to a distinct community?

These subjects are delicate, but it is necessary to contemplate them to teach us to form a true estimate of our situation.

Wars with each other would beget standing armies— a source of more real danger to our liberties than all the power that could be conferred upon the representatives of the union. And wars with each other would lead to opposite alliances with foreign powers, and plunge us into all the labyrinths of European politics....

The application is easy; if there are any foreign enemies, if there are any domestic foes to this country, all their arts and artifices will be employed to effect a dissolution of the union. This cannot be better done than by sowing jealousies of the federal head and cultivating in each state an undue attachment to its own power.

The New York legislature agreed to grant the impost revenue to Congress, but ruled that while the collectors should be accountable to the Continental government they should be appointed by the state. Hamilton had better luck in fighting for the rights of former Tories, many of whom had since pledged their allegiance to the state and some of whom were now members of the assembly itself. As chairman of a committee named to revise the Trespass Act, Hamilton recommended repeal of the article that prevented a defendant from claiming that he had occupied property under military orders. Hamilton's successful argument of his case was reported in the *Daily Advertiser*.

[New York, March 21, 1787]

[Hamilton said:] The courts of justice were at present in a delicate dilemma, obliged either to explain away a positive law of the state or openly violate the national faith by counteracting the very words and spirit of the treaties now in existance. Because the treaty declares a general amnesty, and this state, by this law, declares

that no person shall plead any military order for a trespass committed during the war. He said no state was so
much interested in the due observance of the treaty, as
the state of New-York; the British having possession of
its western frontiers. And which they hold under the
sanction of our not having complied with our national
engagements. He hoped the house would have too much
wisdom, not to do away with this exception; and indeed
he expected the bill would be readily agreed to.

Hamilton was as impatient with "local interests" of his
own state as he was with those of other states. In March, he attempted to
dispose of one of New York's pet projects—the state's claims to the "Hampshire Grants," or what is now the state of Vermont. Although settlers in
this region had effectively asserted their independence in the first years of
the Revolution, New Yorkers still dreamed of reasserting authority over the
area. Hamilton introduced a bill to recognize Vermont's independence
and argued for a more realistic policy.

[New York, March 14, 1787]
I believe there is not a member of this house but considers
the independence of the district [or] territory in question
as a matter fixed and inevitable, all our efforts to a different point have hitherto proved fruitless, and it is long
since we seem to have entirely given up the controversy.
Vermont is in fact *independent,* but she is not *confederated.* And I am constrained to add that the means which
they employ to secure that independence, are objects of
the utmost alarm to the safety of this state, and to the
confederation at large. Are they not wisely inviting and
encouraging settlers by an exemption from taxes, and
availing themselves of the discontents of a neighbouring
state, by turning it to the aggrandizement of their own
power.

Is it not natural to suppose, that a powerful people
both by numbers and situation; unconnected as they now
stand, and without any relative importance in the union.
Irritated by neglect, or stimulated by revenge, I say, is it
not probable under such circumstances they will provide
for their own safety, by seeking connections elsewhere?
And who that hears me doubts, but that these connections have *already* been formed with the British in
Canada.... Whatever may be the present temper of
that people, it is easy to foresee what it will become under

John Lansing

the influence of their leaders. Confederated with a foreign nation, we can be at no loss to anticipate the consequences of such a connection, nor the dangers to this country.... In their present situation they bear no part of our public burdens; if they were a part of the confederacy they must of course participate in them. They are useless to us now, and if they continue as they are, they will be formidable to us hereafter.

Congress had followed the advice of the Annapolis Convention and called on the states to select delegates to meet in Philadelphia in May. Hamilton persuaded the assembly to send a five-man delegation to the convention, but the senate, which had voted down his Vermont bill, refused to send more than three delegates to Philadelphia. A larger delegation could have included some of New York's distinguished nationalists; as it was, the legislature sent Hamilton, John Lansing, and Robert Yates—the last two, good Clintonians. In the last week of the session, Hamilton made a final stand for another factor in the national character when the assembly considered Congress's request that the states pass blanket repeals of all acts "repugnant to the treaty of peace." As in other instances, the assembly followed Hamilton's lead, but the senate ignored the ideas he presented. Hamilton's speech was reported in the *Daily Advertiser.*

[New York, April 17, 1787]

He urged the committee to consent to the passing of the bill, from the consideration, that the state of New-York was the only state to gain any thing by a strict adherence to the treaty. There was no other state in the union that had so much to expect from it.... With respect to the bill as it was drafted in conformity to the recommendation of Congress; he viewed it as a wise, and a salutary measure; one calculated to meet the approbation of the different states, and most likely to answer the end proposed. Were it possible to examine an intricate maze of laws, and to determine which of them, or what parts of laws were opposed to the treaty, it still might not have the intended effect, as different parties would have the judging of this matter. What one should say was a law not inconsistent with the peace, another might say was so, and there would be no end, no decision of the business. Even some of the states might view laws in a different manner. The only way to comply with the treaty, was to make a general and unexceptionable repeal.... He thought it must be obvious to every member of the com-

*A view of Philadelphia in 1777, as
seen from across the Delaware River*

mittee, that as there was no law in direct opposition to the treaty, no difficulty could arise from passing the bill.... He declared that the full operation of the bill, would be no more than merely to declare the treaty the law of the land. And that the judges viewing it as such, shall do away [with] all laws that may appear in direct contravention of it. Treaties were known constitutionally, to be the law of the land, and why be afraid to leave the interpretation of those laws, to the judges; the constitution knows them as the interpreters of the law. He asked if there was any member of the committee that would be willing to see the first treaty of peace ever made by this country violated. This he did not believe, he could not think that any member on that floor harboured such sentiments.

When the legislature voted to hold its next session in Poughkeepsie, Hamilton announced that he would not be a candidate for reelection. If he was reluctant to ride up the Hudson to serve New York, he was quite ready to travel to Philadelphia to serve America. On May 18, he and Yates took their seats at the convention; two weeks later they were joined by John Lansing. In the Philadelphia State House, Hamilton renewed acquaintance with old friends and fellow warriors in the nationalist cause— George Washington, James Madison, Robert and Gouverneur Morris. After Washington was named presiding officer, the convention considered the "Virginia Plan" of government—a plan that provided for a national legislature with representation based on population and an executive and judiciary chosen by the legislators. New Jersey, speaking for the smaller states, presented a series of amendments to the Confederation that would have remedied specific flaws in the old Articles, but would not change the basis of equal representation for all states in the Congress.

Hamilton, who did not agree with either plan, gave the convention his own views in a marathon five-hour speech. Although Hamilton's arguments and the "Plan of Government" that he introduced were not especially influential or persuasive, the speech is historically significant in that it gives the most "correct view" of the form of government that Hamilton felt would be best for America. James Madison recorded Hamilton's oration and afterward, realizing its historical importance, asked Hamilton to check the notes he had taken, to insure their accuracy. As recorded by Madison, Hamilton began by outlining with almost brutal frankness his views of the Confederation in America and of loose confederations in general.

[June 18, 1787]

He was particularly opposed to that [plan] from N. Jersey,

In the engraving above, Washington presides over the Constitutional Convention; below, a plan of the meeting hall, credited to Trumbull.

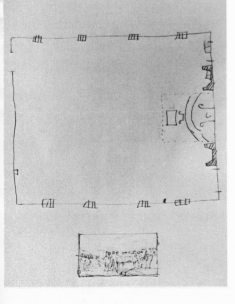

being fully convinced, that no amendment of the Confederation, leaving the States in possession of their Sovereignty could possibly answer the purpose. On the other hand he confessed he was much discouraged by the amazing extent of Country in expecting the desired blessings from any general sovereignty that could be substituted. As to the powers of the Convention, he thought the doubts started on that subject had arisen from distinctions & reasonings too subtle. A *federal* Gov[ernmen]t. he conceived to mean an association of independent Communities into one. Different Confederacies have different powers, and exercise them in different ways. In some instances the powers are exercised over collective bodies; in others over individuals. . . . Great latitude therefore must be given to the signification of the term. . . . He agreed moreover . . . that we owed it to our Country, to do on this emergency whatever we should deem essential to its happiness. The States sent us here to provide for the exigences of the Union. To rely on & propose any plan not adequate to these exigences, merely because it was not clearly within our powers, would be to sacrifice the means to the end. It may be said that the *States* can not *ratify* a plan not within the purview of the article of Confederation providing for alterations & amendments. But may not the States themselves in which no constitutional authority equal to this purpose exists in the Legislatures, have had in view a reference to the people at large. . . .

[Hamilton asserted that the "great question" for the convention was, "What provision shall we make for the happiness of our Country?" Both the Virginia and New Jersey plans, he declared, had serious flaws and did not meet the basic needs of the nation.]

The great & essential principles necessary for the support of Government are 1. an active & constant interest in supporting it. This principle does not exist in the States in favor of the federal Govt. . . . They constantly pursue internal interests adverse to those of the whole. . . . All these when opposed to, invariably prevail over the requisitions & plans of Congress. 2. The love of power. Men love power. The same remarks are applicable to this principle. The States have constantly shewn a disposition rather to regain the powers delegated by them than to part with more, or to give effect to what they had parted with. The ambition of their demagogues is known to hate the controul of the Genl. Government....3. An habitual attachment of the people. The whole force of this tie is on the side of the State Govt. Its sovereignty is immediately before the eyes of the people; its protection is immediately enjoyed by them. From its hand... all those acts which familiarize & endear Govt. to a people, are dispensed to them. 4. *Force* by which may be understood a *coertion of laws* or *coertion of arms.* Cong[res]s. have not the former except in few cases. In particular States, this coercion is nearly sufficient; tho'...in most cases, not entirely so. A certain portion of military force is absolutely necessary in large communities....But how can this force be exerted on the States collectively. It is impossible. It amounts to a war between the parties. Foreign powers also will not be idle spectators....5. *influence.* he did not mean corruption, but a dispensation of those regular honors & emoluments, which produce an attachment to the Govt. Almost all the weight of these is on the side of the States; and must continue so as long as the States continue to exist. All the passions then we see, of avarice, ambition, interest, which govern most individuals, and all public bodies, fall into the current of the States, and do not flow in the stream of the Genl. Govt. The former therefore will generally be an overmatch for the Genl. Govt. and render any confederacy, in its very nature precarious.

Continuing his oration, Hamilton presented historical examples of the failure of confederacies, closely analyzed the British system of government, and discoursed on the nature of executive power. He then offered his colleagues his plan for an American government. His draft of that plan has survived and is printed here in full. Hamilton's ideal, however, was far removed from the practical compromises that the convention worked into the Constitution of 1787.

[Philadelphia, June 18, 1787]

I   The Supreme Legislative Power of the United States of America to be vested in two distinct bodies of men— the one to be called the *Assembly* the other the *senate*; who together shall form the Legislature of the United States, with power to pass all *laws whatsoever,* subject

Hamilton's notes for his speech proposing a plan of government

to the *negative* hereafter mentioned.

II The Assembly to consist of persons elected *by the People* to serve for three years.

III The Senate to consist of persons elected to serve during *good behaviour*. Their election to be made by *Electors* chosen for that purpose by the People. In order to this The States to be divided into election districts. On the death removal or resignation of any senator his place to be filled out of the district from which he came.

IV The Supreme Executive authority of the United States to be vested in a *governor* to be elected to serve *during good behaviour*. His election to be made by *Electors* chosen by *electors* chosen by the people in the election districts aforesaid or by electors chosen for that purpose by the respective legislatures—provided that [if] an election be not made within a limited time the President of the Senate shall...be the Governor. The Governor to have a *negative* upon all laws about to be passed and to have the execution of all laws passed—to be the Commander in Chief of the land and naval forces and of the Militia of the United States—to have the direction of war, when authorised or began—to have with the *advice* and *approbation* of the Senate the power of making all treaties—to have the appointment of the *heads or chief* officers of the departments of finance war and foreign affairs—to have the *nomination* of all other officers (ambassadors to foreign nations included) subject to the approbation or rejection of the Senate—to have the power of pardoning all offences but *treason*, which he shall not pardon without the approbation of the Senate.

V On the death resignation or removal of the Governor his authorities to be exercised by the President of the Senate.

VI The Senate to have the sole power of *declaring war*—the power of advising and approving all treaties—the power of approving or rejecting all appointments of officers except the heads or chiefs of the departments of finance war and foreign affairs.

VII The Supreme Judicial authority of the United States to be vested in twelve Judges, to hold their offices during good behaviour with adequate and permanent salaries. This Court to have original jurisdiction in all causes of capture and an appellative jurisdiction (from the Courts of the several states) in all causes in which the revenues of the general government or the citizens of foreign nations are concerned.

VIII   The Legislature of the United States to have power to institute Courts in each state for the determination of all causes of capture and of all matters relating to their revenues, or in which the citizens of foreign nations are concerned.

IX   The Governor Senators and all Officers of the United States to be liable to impeachment for mal and corrupt conduct, and upon conviction to be removed from office and disqualified for holding any place of trust or profit. All impeachments to be tried by a Court to consist of the judges of the Supreme Court chief or Senior Judge of the superior Court of law of each state — provided that such judge hold his place during good behaviour and have a permanent salary.

X   All laws of the particular states contrary to the constitution or laws of the United States to be utterly void. And the better to prevent such laws being passed the Governor or President of each state shall *be appointed by the general government* and shall have a *negative* upon the laws about to be passed in the state of which he is governor or President.

XI   No state to have any forces land or naval — and the *Militia* of all the states to be under the sole and *exclusive direction* of the United States *the officers* of which to be appointed and commissioned by them.

William Paterson, who proposed the "New Jersey Plan" of government on behalf of the smaller states

After reading his Plan of Government to the delegates, Hamilton concluded with these remarks, which were jotted down by his colleague Robert Yates.

[Philadelphia, June 18, 1787]
I confess that this plan and that from Virginia are very remote from the idea of the people. Perhaps the Jersey plan is nearest their expectation. But the people are gradually ripening in their opinions of government — they begin to be tired of an excess of democracy — and

what even is the Virginia plan, but pork still, with a little change of the sauce.

Although the delegates chose to use the Virginia Plan rather than Hamilton's as the basis for their debates, they did not forget what he had proposed on June 18. "Small-state" men were especially alarmed by his remarks. As the members of the convention discussed the proposition that "a National Government ought to be established," Madison recorded Hamilton's attempts to placate these representatives.

[Philadelphia, June 19, 1787]

[Hamilton] took this occasion of observing for the purpose of appeasing the fears of the small States, that two circumstances would render them secure under a National Govt. in which they might lose the equality of rank they now held: one was the local situation of the 3 largest States Virga. Masts. & Pa. They were separated from each other by distance of place, and equally so, by all the peculiarities which distinguish the interests of one State from those of another. No combination therefore could be dreaded. In the second place, as there was a gradation in the States from Va. the largest down to Delaware the smallest, it would always happen that ambitious combinations among a few States might & w[oul]d. be counteracted by defensive combinations of greater extent among the rest. No combination has been seen among large Counties merely as such, ag[ain]st. lesser Counties. The more close the Union of the States, and the more compleat the authority of the whole: the less opportunity will be allowed the stronger States to injure the weaker.

Edmund Randolph, who put forward the "Virginia Plan" of government

As the convention began to consider the upper house of the new Congress, Hamilton realized that his proposal for a Senate with life terms would not be accepted, but he joined James Madison in arguing for as long a term for Senators as possible. Again, the notes on the debate are Madison's.

[Philadelphia, June 26, 1787]

He [Hamilton] concurred with Mr. Madison in thinking we were now to decide for ever the fate of Republican Government; and that if we did not give to that form due stability and wisdom, it would be disgraced & lost among ourselves, disgraced & lost to mankind for ever.

He acknowledged himself not to think favorably of Republican Government; but addressed his remarks to those who did think favorably of it, in order to prevail on them to tone their Government as high as possible. He professed himself to be as zealous an advocate for liberty as any man whatever, and trusted he should be as willing a martyr to it though he differed as to the form in which it was most eligible.

The hardest problem to be solved, however, was not the length of the Senators' terms, but the basis on which Senate seats would be distributed. The Virginia Plan proposed that seats in both houses be assigned in proportion to population; smaller states demanded protection for state interests in at least one part of the national legislature. Hamilton spoke on behalf of a Senate with a "popular" base, not equal representation for all states. Madison recorded his remarks.

[Philadelphia, June 29, 1787]

. . . as States are a collection of individual men which ought we to respect most, the rights of the people composing them, or of the artificial beings resulting from the composition. Nothing could be more preposterous or absurd than to sacrifice the former to the latter. It has been s[ai]d. that if the smaller States renounce their *equality*, they renounce at the same time their *liberty*. The truth is it is a contest for power, not for liberty. Will the men composing the small States be less free than those composing the larger. The State of Delaware having 40,000 souls will *lose power*, if she has 1/10 only of the votes allowed to Pa. having 400,000: but will the people of Del: *be less free*, if each citizen has an equal vote with each citizen of Pa. . . .

[Hamilton warned that this was a "critical moment" that demanded all the wisdom the delegates possessed.]

It had been said that respectability in the eyes of foreign Nations was not the object at which we aimed; that the proper object of republican Government was domestic tranquility & happiness. This was an ideal distinction. No Governmt. could give us tranquility & happiness at home, which did not possess sufficient stability and strength to make us respectable abroad. This was the critical moment for forming such a Government. We

A view of Philadelphia's New Market

174

should run every risk in trusting to future amendments. As yet we retain the habits of union. We are weak & sensible of our weakness. Henceforward the motives will become feebler, and the difficulties greater. It is a miracle that we were now here exercising our tranquil & free deliberations on the subject. It would be madness to trust to future miracles. A thousand causes must obstruct a reproduction of them.

Later that day, Hamilton left the convention to return to his business affairs in New York. Although his own ideas on government had met a cool reception, he had not lost interest in the proceedings in Philadelphia, as he made clear in a letter to George Washington.

[New York, July 3, 1787]

In my passage through the Jerseys and since my arrival here I have taken particular pains to discover the public sentiment and I am more and more convinced that this is the critical opportunity for establishing the prosperity of this country on a solid foundation. I have conversed with men of information not only of this City but from different parts of the state; and they agree that there has been an astonishing revolution for the better in the minds of the people. The prevailing apprehension among thinking men is that the Convention, from a fear of shocking the popular opinion, will not go far enough. They seem to be convinced that a strong well mounted government will better suit the popular palate than one of a different complexion. Men in office are indeed taking all possible pains to give an unfavourable impression of the Convention; but the current seems to be running strongly the other way.

A plain but sensible man, in a conversation I had with him yesterday, expressed himself nearly in this manner. The people begin to be convinced that their "excellent form of government" as they have been used to call it, will not answer their purpose; and that they must substitute something not very remote from that which they have lately quitted.

These appearances though they will not warrant a conclusion that the people are yet ripe for such a plan as I advocate, yet serve to prove that there is no reason to despair of their adopting one equally energetic, if the Convention should think proper to propose it. They serve to prove that we ought not to allow too much weight to objections drawn from the supposed repugnancy of the people to an efficient constitution....

Not having compared ideas with you, Sir, I cannot judge how far our sentiments agree; but...my anxiety for the event of the deliberations of the Convention induces me to make this communication of what appears to be the tendency of the public mind. I own to you Sir that I am seriously and deeply distressed at the aspect of the Councils which prevailed when I left Philadelphia. I fear that we shall let slip the golden opportunity of rescuing the American empire from disunion anarchy and misery. No motley or feeble measure can answer the end or will finally receive the public support. Decision is true wisdom and will be not less reputable to the Convention than salutary to the community.

Having spent the summer looking after his law practice, Hamilton returned to Philadelphia in the first week of September to find that most of the questions concerning the new plan of government had been settled. One major problem remained—the election of the President. The Committee of Detail, appointed in July, had suggested a Chief Executive chosen by the national legislature for a seven-year term. Another committee, appointed September 4, proposed that he be named instead by electors chosen in each state. Hamilton's presentation of his own view was recorded by Madison.

[Philadelphia, September 6, 1787]

Mr. HAMILTON said that he had been restrained from entering into the discussions by his dislike of the Scheme of Govt. in General; but as he meant to support the plan to be recommended, as better than nothing, he wished in this place to offer a few remarks. He liked the new modification, on the whole, better than that in the printed Report [made by the Committee of Detail]. In this the President was a Monster elected for seven years, and ineligible afterwards; having great powers, in appointments to office, & continually tempted by this constitutional disqualification to abuse them in order to subvert the Government. Although he should be made re-eligible, still if appointed by the Legislature, he would be tempted to make use of corrupt influence to be continued in office. It seemed peculiarly desireable therefore that some other mode of election should be devised. Con-

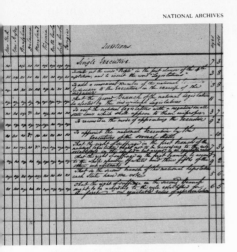

*A voting record kept during
the Constitutional Convention*

sidering the different views of different States, & the different districts Northern Middle & Southern, he concurred with those who thought that the votes would not be concentered, and that the appointment would consequently in the present mode devolve on the Senate. The nomination to offices will give great weight to the President. Here then is a mutual connection & influence, that will perpetuate the President, and aggrandize both him & the Senate. What is to be the remedy? He saw none better than to let the highest number of ballots, whether a majority or not, appoint the President. What was the objection to this? Merely that too small a number might appoint. But as the plan stands, the Senate may take the candidate having the smallest number of votes, and make him President.

The convention agreed with Hamilton that this modification—the basis of the Electoral College—was preferable. On September 10, Elbridge Gerry of Massachusetts suggested a change in the article concerning future amendments to the Constitution. As it stood, amendments could come only when two thirds of the states applied to Congress, and Gerry feared that a majority of the states might make alterations "that may subvert the State-Constitutions altogether." Hamilton seconded Gerry's motion, but explained that he did so for quite different reasons.

[Philadelphia, September 10, 1787]

It had been wished by many and was much to have been desired that an easier mode for introducing amendments had been provided by the articles of Confederation It was equally desireable now that an easy mode should be established for supplying defects which will probably appear in the New System The mode proposed was not adequate. The State Legislatures will not apply for alterations but with a view to increase their own powers. The National Legislature will be the first to perceive and will be the most sensible to the necessity of amendments, and ought also to be empowered, whenever two thirds of each branch should concur to call a Convention. There could be no danger in giving this power, as the people would finally decide in the case.

After the delegates agreed to the articles of the new Constitution, problems of protocol still remained. There was, of course, the delicate question of the manner in which the Constitution should be ratified. When Elbridge Gerry demanded that Congress be given the opportunity to pass on the Constitution, Hamilton supported him. For the second time on September 10, Hamilton spoke on behalf of one of Gerry's motions, but again for very different reasons from those that had motivated the Massachusetts delegate.

Elbridge Gerry of Massachusetts

[Philadelphia, September 10, 1787]

Mr. HAMILTON concurred with Mr. Gerry as to the indecorum of not requiring the approbation of Congress. He considered this as a necessary ingredient in the transaction. He thought it wrong also to allow nine States ... to institute a new Government on the ruins of the existing one. He wd. propose as a better modification ... that the plan should be sent to Congress in order that the same if approved by them, may be communicated to the State Legislatures, to the end that they may refer it to State Conventions; each Legislature declaring that if the Convention of the State should think the plan ought to take effect among nine ratifying States, the same shd. take effect accordingly.

By September 17, the last day of the convention, many of the delegates had already left Philadelphia. Some who had remained were so bitterly opposed to the Constitution that had been approved that they refused to add their signatures to the document. Hamilton presented his arguments in favor of signing.

[Philadelphia, September 17, 1787]

Mr. HAMILTON expressed his anxiety that every member should sign. A few characters of consequence, by opposing or even refusing to sign the Constitution, might do infinite mischief by kindling the latent sparks which lurk under an enthusiasm in favor of the Convention which may soon subside. No man's ideas were more remote from the plan than his were known to be; but is it possible to deliberate between anarchy and Convulsion on one side, and the chance of good to be expected from the plan on the other.

In the two weeks following the convention's adjournment, Hamilton jotted down some "Conjectures about the New Constitution," in which he weighed the chances for ratification of the document by the various states.

Hamilton was the only New York
delegate to sign the Constitution.

[September 17–30, 1787]

The new constitution has in favour of its success these circumstances—a very great weight of influence of the persons who framed it, particularly in the universal popularity of General Washington—the good will of the commercial interest throughout the states which will give all its efforts to the establishment of a government capable of regulating protecting and extending the commerce of the Union—the good will of most men of property in the several states who wish a government of the union able to protect them against domestic violence and the depredations which the democratic spirit is apt to make on property; and who are besides anxious for the respectability of the nation—the hopes of the Creditors of the United States that a general government possessing the means of doing it will pay the debt of the Union—a strong belief in the people at large of the insufficiency of the present confederation to preserve the existence of the Union and of the necessity of the union to their safety and prosperity; of course a strong desire of a change and a predisposition to receive well the propositions of the Convention....

But the causes operating against its adoption are powerful and there will be nothing astonishing in the Contrary.

If it do not finally obtain, it is probable the discussion of the question will beget such struggles animosities and heats in the community that this circumstance conspiring with the *real necessity* of an essential change in our present situation will produce civil war. Should this happen, whatever parties prevail it is probable governments very different from the present in their principles will be established. A dismemberment of the Union and monarchies in different portions of it may be expected. It may however happen that no civil war will take place; but several republican confederacies be established between different combinations of the particular states....

If the government be adopted, it is probable general Washington will be the President of the United States. This will insure a wise choice of men to administer the government and a good administration. A good administration will conciliate the confidence and affection of the people and perhaps enable the government to acquire more consistency than the proposed constitution seems to promise for so great a Country. It may then triumph altogether over the state governments and reduce them to an intire subordination, dividing the larger states into smaller districts. . . .

If this should not be the case, in the course of a few years, it is probable that the contests about the boundaries of power between the particular governments and the general government and the *momentum* of the larger states in such contests will produce a dissolution of the Union. This after all seems to be the most likely result.

But it is almost arrogance in so complicated a subject, depending so intirely on the incalculable fluctuations of the human passions, to attempt even a conjecture about the event.

There was one element in the battle for ratification that was not subject to "conjecture"—the bitter opposition of Governor George Clinton of New York. In July, after having left Philadelphia, Hamilton learned that Clinton had "in public company" criticized the convening of the Constitutional Convention and declared that "the result of their deliberations, whatever it might be, would only serve to throw the community into confusion." In an anonymous letter published in the *Daily Advertiser*, Hamilton offered the governor "the following reflections."

[New York, July 21, 1787]

First. That from the almost universal concurrence of the states in the measure of appointing a Convention, and from the powers given to their Deputies . . . it appears clearly to be the general sense of America, that the present confederation *is not* "equal to the purposes of the union," but requires material alterations.

Secondly. That the concurrence of the legislatures of twelve out of the thirteen states . . . in a measure of so extraordinary a complexion, the direct object of which is the abridgement of their own power, in favor of a general government, is of itself a strong presumptive proof that there exist real evils; and that these evils are of so extensive and cogent a nature, as to have been capable of giving an impulse from one extremity of the United States to the other. . . .

[Hamilton then went on to itemize these "evils," which had crippled the American economy and degraded "our national character and consequence" to such an extent that "the very existence of the union is in imminent danger." He closed with a personal attack on Clinton.]

The residence of Governor Clinton on Pearl Street in lower Manhattan

Eighthly. That however justifiable it might be in the governor to oppose the appointment of a convention, if the measure were still under deliberation; and if he sincerely believed it to be a pernicious one, yet the general voice of America having decided in its favor, it is *unwarrantable* and *culpable in any man*, in so serious a posture of our national affairs, to endeavour to prepossess the public mind against the hitherto undetermined and unknown measures of a body to whose councils America has, in a great measure, entrusted its future fate, and to whom the people in general look up, under the blessing of heaven, for their political salvation.

Ninthly. That such conduct in a man high in office, argues greater attachment to his *own power* than to the *public good*, and furnishes strong reason to suspect a dangerous predetermination to oppose whatever may tend to diminish the *former*, however it may promote the *latter.*

If there be any man among us, who acts so unworthy a part, it becomes a free and enlightened people to observe him with a jealous eye, and when he sounds the alarm of danger from another quarter, to examine whether they have not more to apprehend from *himself.*

After Hamilton returned to his duties in Philadelphia, "A Republican" replied to his charges against Clinton. The *Daily Advertiser* carried Hamilton's rebuttal, in which he disputed the claim that printing Clinton's remarks was "calculated to produce the evil pretended to be guarded against."

[New York, September 15, 1787]

If his Excellency was predetermined to oppose the measures of the Convention, as his conduct indicates, he would take care himself to propagate his sentiments, in the manner in which it could be done with the most effect. This appears to have been his practice. It was therefore proper that the antidote should go along with the poison; and that the community should be apprised, that he was capable of forming such a predetermination, before, it can be presumed, he had any knowlege of the measures themselves, on which to found his judgment.

181

A cry is attempted to be raised against the publication ... as if it were an invasion of the right of the first Magistrate of the State to deliver his sentiments on a matter of public concern. The fallacy of this artifice will easily be detected. The Governor has an undoubted right to give his sentiments freely on every public measure.... But every *right* may be abused by a *wrong exercise* of it.... The only question then is, whether he has in the present instance used his right properly, or improperly—whether it became him, by *anticipation*, to endeavour to prejudice the community against the "unknown and undetermined" measures of a body, to which the general voice of the union had delegated the important trust of concerting and proposing a plan for reforming the national constitution? Let every man answer this question to himself.

The apologists for the Governor, in the intemperate ardor of their zeal for his character, seem to forget another *right*, very precious to the citizens of a free country, *that* of examing the conduct of their rulers....

But, observations of either kind might mutually have been spared. There is no danger that the rights of a man, at the head of the Government (possessing all the influence to be derived from long continuance in office, the disposition of lucrative places, and *consummate talents* for popularity) can be injured by the voice of a private individual. There is as little danger, that the spirit of the people of this State will ever tolerate attempts to seduce, to awe, or to clamor them out of the privilege of bringing the conduct of men in power to the bar of public examination.

Hamilton's public career in the first nine months of 1787 ended, as it had begun, with an attack upon George Clinton. By September of that year Hamilton had already begun concentrating his energies on winning the ratification of the Federal Constitution—an issue that would cause statewide differences, that would lead to the creation of rival political organizations, and that would influence the course of state and national history for years to come. The time had come for Hamilton the Continentalist to become Hamilton the Federalist.

Chapter 7

The Federalist

O f all the compromises involved in the creation of the Constitution, few
were as remarkable as Alexander Hamilton's bargain with his own
principles. Although "no man's ideas were more remote from the plan"
than his, no man worked harder to see that the plan succeeded. Since
the Constitution would not take effect until two thirds of the states had
ratified it, Hamilton and his allies had to fight for the Federalist cause on
several fronts.

Their first victory came in appropriating the name Federalist. Originally,
the term had been applied to defenders of the Articles of Confederation, but
it was now being used by those who sought to replace the "federal" form of
government with the "national" regime promised under the new Constitution. Supporters of the federal plan, who opposed the Constitution, complained that they were unfairly labeled Antifederalists. They could do
nothing but grumble, however, for Hamilton had laid his party's claim to
the Federalist title in the public press. *The Federalist* papers, a series of
more than eighty essays produced between October 27, 1787, and
May 28, 1788, presented the definitive defense of the new Constitution
and the political theories of its supporters. Signed "Publius," the essays
were written in collaboration first with John Jay and later with James
Madison, but since Hamilton himself produced two thirds of these articles,
as well as arranging for their publication and distribution, he had time for
little else in the eight months following the Philadelphia Convention.

During these first months after the Constitution was submitted to the
states, Hamilton's words were primarily written for or spoken to the public.
Few of the documents that appear in this chapter are reprinted from manuscripts in Hamilton's own hand. His drafts of *The Federalist* essays have
vanished, and only rough outlines of his speeches have survived. Historians
must rely on printed versions of the "Publius" articles and on newspaper
reports and other records of his orations. What little private correspondence

Hamilton engaged in at this time also deals primarily with the increasingly bitter dispute over ratification. Particularly troublesome was the whispered campaign launched against him by the Clintonians. By October, 1787, the attack had become so harsh that Hamilton turned to Washington for aid.

[New York, October 11–15, 1787]

Among many contemptible artifices practiced by them, they have had recourse to an insinuation that I *palmed* myself upon you and that you *dismissed* me from your family. This I confess hurts my feelings, and if it obtains credit, will require a contradiction.

You...know how destitute of foundation such insinuations are. My confidence in your justice will not permit me to doubt your readiness to put the matter in its true light in your answer to this letter....

The New Constitution is as popular in this City as it is possible for any thing to be—and the prospect thus far is favourable to it throughout the state. But there is no saying what turn things may take when the flood of official influence is let loose against it. This is to be expected, for though the Governor has not publicly declared himself his particular connections and confidential friends are loud against it.

Washington replied promptly, asserting that both charges were "entirely unfounded," but he also expressed his "unfeigned concern" over the bitter division between Hamilton and Clinton. When Hamilton answered Washington, he did not raise the point again.

[New York, October 30, 1787]

I am much obliged to Your Excellency for the explicit manner in which you contradict the insinuations mentioned in my last letter. The only use I shall make of your answer will be to put it into the hands of a few friends.

The constitution proposed has in this state warm friends and warm enemies. The first impressions every where are in its favour; but the artillery of its opponents makes some impression. The event cannot yet be foreseen. The inclosed is the first number of a series of papers to be written in its defence.

The paper sent to Washington was the first of *The Federalist* essays. On Saturday, October 27, readers of New York's *Inde-*

pendent Journal: or, the General Advertiser were introduced to "Publius," whose object was to persuade voters to elect Federalist (that is, pro-Constitution) delegates to the state's ratifying convention.

[New York, October 27, 1787]

To the People of the State of New York.

AFTER an unequivocal experience of the inefficacy of the subsisting Fœderal Government, you are called upon to deliberate on a new Constitution for the United States of America. The subject speaks its own importance; comprehending in its consequences, nothing less than the existence of the UNION, the safety and welfare of the parts of which it is composed, the fate of an empire, in many respects, the most interesting the world. It has been frequently remarked, that it seems to have been reserved to the people of this country, by their conduct and example, to decide the important question, whether societies of men are really capable or not, of establishing good government from ref[l]ection and choice, or whether they are forever destined to depend, for their political constitutions, on accident and force. If there be any truth in the remark, the crisis, at which we are arrived, may with propriety be regarded as the æra in which that decision is to be made; and a wrong election of the part we shall act, may, in this view, deserve to be considered as the general misfortune of mankind....

...My Countrymen, I own to you, that, after having given it an attentive consideration, I am clearly of opinion, it is your interest to adopt [the new Constitution]. I am convinced, that this is the safest course for your liberty, your dignity, and your happiness....I will not amuse you with an appearance of deliberation, when I have decided. I frankly acknowledge to you my convictions, and I will freely lay before you the reasons on which they are founded....

I propose in a series of papers to discuss the following interesting particulars—*The utility of the* UNION *to your political prosperity—The insufficiency of the present Confederation to preserve that Union—The necessity of a government at least equally energetic with the one proposed to the attainment of this object—The conformity of the proposed constitution to the true principles of republican government—Its analogy to your own state constitution—and lastly, The additional security, which*

The Independent Journal *was one of the New York papers in which* The Federalist *essays first appeared.*

its adoption will afford to the preservation of that species of government, to liberty and to property.

The extent of Hamilton's contributions to *The Federalist* makes it impossible to include even a representative sampling of these essays. A substantial portion of *No. 13*, however, the shortest of Hamilton's pieces, is reprinted here to give an idea of their content and style. In this article, Publius was still concerned with "the utility of the UNION," this time in matters of "œconomy."

[New York, November 28, 1787]

If the States are united under one government, there will be but one national civil list to support; if they are divided into several confederacies, there will be as many different national civil lists to be provided for.... The entire separation of the States into thirteen unconnected sovereignties is a project too extravagant and too replete with danger to have many advocates. The ideas of men who speculate upon the dismemberment of the empire, seem generally turned towards three confederacies; one consisting of the four northern, another of the four middle, and a third of the five southern States. There is little probability that there would be a greater number. According to this distribution each confederacy would comprise an extent of territory larger than that of the kingdom of Great-Britain. No well informed man will suppose that the affairs of such a confederacy can be properly regulated by a government, less comprehensive in its organs or institutions, than that, which has been proposed by the Convention. When the dimensions of a State attain to a certain magnitude, it requires the same energy of government and the same terms of administration; which are requisite in one of much greater extent. This idea admits not of precise demonstration, because there is no rule by which we can measure the momentum of civil power, necessary to the government of any given number of individuals; but when we consider that the island of Britain, nearly commensurate with each of the supposed confederacies, contains about eight millions of people, and when we reflect upon the degree of authority required to direct the passions of so large a society to the public good, we shall see no reason to doubt that the like portion of power would be sufficient to perform the same task in

Hamilton's bookplate

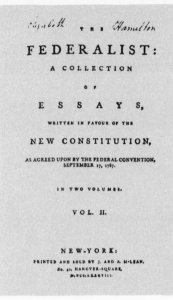

The title page of Volume II of The Federalist *papers, bearing the name of Elizabeth Hamilton*

a society far more numerous. Civil power properly organised and exerted is capable of diffusing its force to a very great extent; and can in a manner reproduce itself in every part of a great empire by a judicious arrangement of subordinate institutions....

If in addition to the consideration of a plurality of civil lists, we take into view the number of persons who must necessarily be employed to guard the inland communication, between the different confederacies, against illicit trade, and who in time will infallibly spring up out of the necessities of revenue; and if we also take into view the military establishments, which it has been shewn would unavoidably result from the jealousies and conflicts of the several nations, into which the States would be divided, we shall clearly discover, that a separation would be not less injurious to the œconomy than to the tranquillity, commerce, revenue and liberty of every part.

PUBLIUS

By April, 1788, six states had ratified the Constitution. James Madison had departed from New York in March to prepare for his work in the Virginia Convention, leaving Hamilton to supervise the publication of the remaining *Federalist* essays. There were some difficulties in literary collaboration by mail, as this letter to Madison shows.

[New York, April 3, 1788]

I think...the principles we have talked of, in respect to the legislative authorities, are not only just but will apply to the other departments. Nor will the consequences appear so disagreeable, as they may seem at first sight, when we attend to the true import of the rule established. The states *retain* all the authorities they were *before* possessed of, not alienated in the three modes pointed out; but this does not include cases which are the *creatures* of the New Constitution. For instance, the crime of treason against the United States *immediately*, is a crime known only to the New Constitution. There of course *was* no power in the state constitutions to pardon that crime. There will therefore be none under the new &c. This or something like it seems to me to afford the best solution of the difficulty.

I send you the Fœderalist from the beginning to the conclusion of the commentary on the Executive branch. If

187

our suspicions of the author be right, he must be too much engaged to make a rapid progress in what remains....

We are told that your election has succeeded; with which we all felicitate ourselves. I will thank you for an account of the result generally.

In this state our prospects are much as you left them — a moot point which side will prevail. Our friends to the Northward are active.

Between April 2 and May 28, 1788, Publius was silent. Involved with his legal work and with the outcome of elections in other states, Hamilton was also worried about the election of delegates in New York, where the Antifederalists had built a strong statewide organization of county committees. Votes were cast on the last Tuesday in April, and the results showed that *The Federalist* papers had had little effect on "the People of the State of New York," to whom they were addressed. As one New Yorker remarked, Publius was not "intelligible to the common people." Hamilton, Jay, and Robert R. Livingston were easy winners in Manhattan. But, as Hamilton wrote to Madison in mid-May, it was clear that Clinton's forces had triumphed upstate.

[New York, May 19, 1788]

Some days since I wrote to you, My Dear Sir....

I then mentioned to you that the question of a majority for or against the constitution would depend upon the County of Albany. By the latter accounts from that quarter I fear much that the issue there has been against us.

As Clinton is truly the leader of his party, and is inflexibly obstinate I count little on overcoming opposition by reason. Our only chances will be the previous ratification by nine states, which may shake the firmness of his followers; and a change in the sentiments of the people which have been for some time travelling towards the constitution, though the first impressions made by every species of influence and artifice were too strong to be eradicated in time to give a decisive turn to the elections. We shall leave nothing undone to cultivate a favourable disposition in the citizens at large.

The language of the Antifœderalists is that if all the other states adopt, New York ought still to hold out. I have the most direct intelligence, but in a manner, which forbids a public use being made of it, that Clinton has in several conversations declared his opinion of the *inutility* of the UNION. Tis an unhappy reflection, that

During the election campaign of 1788, Hamilton and eight other Federalists addressed this broadside to New York's voters.

the friends to it should by quarrelling for straws among themselves promote the designs of its adversaries.

We think here that the situation of your state is critical. Let me know what you now think of it. I believe you meet nearly at the time we do. It will be of vast importance that an exact communication should be kept up between us at that period; and the moment *any decisive* question is taken, if favourable, I request you to dispatch an express to me with pointed orders to make all possible diligence, by changing horses &c. All expences shall be thankfully and liberally paid.

The final results of the New York election showed the Federalists defeated by a margin of more than two to one. They won only nineteen contests in four counties, while the Antifederalists won forty-six elections in nine counties. Despite this setback, however, Hamilton could approach the last *Federalist* essays with a degree of optimism. When he wrote the first number, no state convention had met to consider the Constitution; but by the time the last essays were published on May 28, 1788, seven states had ratified the new system, and by the end of May, an eighth had given its assent. Furthermore, few Antifederalists still felt that the Constitution should be rejected out of hand, arguing instead that the new government would be palatable only if it contained some protection for individual rights and civil liberties. Amid this new climate of opinion, Hamilton altered his approach in his last essays. Although a "bill of rights" had been discussed for several months, Hamilton did not mention its absence from the Constitution until the eighty-fourth *Federalist*, the next to last in the series.

[New York, May 28, 1788]

The opposers of the new system in this state, who profess an unlimited admiration for its constitution, are among the most intemperate partizans of a bill of rights. To justify their zeal in this matter, they alledge two things; one is, that...the constitution of New-York ...contains in the body of it various provisions in favour of particular privileges and rights, which in substance amount to the same thing; the other is, that the constitution adopts in their full extent the common and statute law of Great-Britain, by which many other rights not expressed in it are equally secured.

To the first I answer, that the constitution proposed by the convention contains, as well as the constitution of this state, a number of such provisions....

*A copy, by the secretary of the
New York senate, of the resolution
appointing Hamilton a delegate to
Congress for the year 1788*

To the second, that is, to the pretended establishment of the common and statute law by the constitution, I answer, that they are expressly made subject "to such alterations and provisions as the legislature shall from time to time make concerning the same." They are therefore at any moment liable to repeal by the ordinary legislative power, and of course have no constitutional sanction....

[Further, Hamilton argued, an explicit bill of rights could endanger the liberties it was designed to protect.]

Why for instance, should it be said, that the liberty of the press shall not be restrained, when no power is given by which restrictions may be imposed?...it would furnish, to men disposed to usurp, a plausible pretence for claiming that power. They might urge with a semblance of reason, that the constitution ought not to be charged with the absurdity of providing against the abuse of an authority, which was not given, and that the provision against restraining the liberty of the press afforded a clear implication, that a power to prescribe proper regulations concerning it, was intended to be vested in the national government....

There remains but one other view of this matter to conclude the point. The truth is, after all the declamation we have heard, that the constitution is itself in every rational sense, and to every useful purpose, A BILL OF RIGHTS. The several bills of rights, in Great-Britain, form its constitution, and conversely the constitution of each state is its bill of rights. And the proposed constitution, if adopted, will be the bill of rights of the union. Is it one object of a bill of rights to declare and specify the political privileges of the citizens in the structure and administration of the government? This is done in the most ample and precise manner in the plan of the convention....Is another object of a bill of rights to define certain immunities and modes of proceeding, which are relative to personal and private concerns? This we have seen has also been attended to...in the same plan. Adverting therefore to the substantial meaning of a bill of rights, it is absurd to allege that it is not to be found in the work of the convention....It certainly must be immaterial what mode is observed as to the order of declaring the rights of the citizens, if they are to be found in any part of the instrument which establishes the government.

Hamilton's reasons for opposing a bill of rights became clear in the last *Federalist*. Advocates of the measure had seized upon the idea of incorporating these amendments as "previous conditions" to ratification by the states that had not yet acted. Hamilton believed that he could not afford to strengthen the Antifederalist cause by admitting that there was any merit in their arguments.

[New York, May 28, 1788]

Concessions on the part of the friends of the plan, that it has not a claim to absolute perfection, have afforded matter of no small triumph to its enemies. Why, say they, should we adopt an imperfect thing? Why not amend it, and make it perfect before it is irrevocably established? This may be plausible enough, but it is only plausible. In the first place I remark, that the extent of these concessions has been greatly exaggerated.... No advocate of the measure can be found who will not declare his sentiment, that the system, though it may not be perfect in every part, is upon the whole a good one, is the best that the present views and circumstances of the country will permit, and is such an one as promises every species of security which a reasonable people can desire....

[In closing the *Federalist* series, Hamilton quoted the British political scientist David Hume, who had written that "no human genius" could, alone, establish an effective government for "a large state or society."]

"The judgments of many must unite in the work: EXPERIENCE must guide their labour: Time must bring it to perfection: And the FEELING of inconveniences must correct the mistakes which they *inevitably* fall into, in their first trials and experiments." These judicious reflections contain a lesson of moderation to all the sincere lovers of the union, and ought to put them upon their guard against hazarding anarchy, civil war, a perpetual alienation of the states from each other, and perhaps the military despotism of a victorious demagogue, in the pursuit of what they are not likely to obtain, but from TIME

New York State's coat of arms

and EXPERIENCE. It may be in me a defect of political fortitude, but I acknowledge, that I cannot entertain an equal
tranquillity with those who affect to treat the dangers of
a longer continuance in our present situation as imaginary.
A NATION without a NATIONAL GOVERNMENT is, in my view,
an awful spectacle. The establishment of a constitution,
in time of profound peace, by the voluntary consent of a
whole people, is a PRODIGY, to the completion of which I
look forward with trembling anxiety. I can reconcile it
to no rules of prudence to let go the hold we now have,
in so arduous an enterprise, upon seven out of the
thirteen states; and after having passed over so considerable a part of the ground to recommence the
course. I dread the more the consequences of new
attempts, because I KNOW that POWERFUL INDIVIDUALS,
in this and in other states, are enemies to a general
national government, in every possible shape.

Federalist strategy at the New York Convention that
was to meet at Poughkeepsie in mid-June depended on the success of the
Constitution elsewhere. Hamilton had already made arrangements for
obtaining reports from the Virginia Convention. New Hampshire's convention had met in February, adjourned without taking action on the Constitution, and was to reconvene in June. Early in that month Hamilton outlined
his plans to John Sullivan, a New Hampshire Federalist.

New York, June 6, 1788.
You will no doubt have understood that the Antifederal
party has prevailed in this State by a large majority.
It is therefore of the utmost importance that all external
circumstances should be made use of to influence their
conduct. This will suggest to you the *great advantage* of
a speedy decision in your State, if you can be sure of
the question, and a prompt communication of the event
to us. With this view, permit me to request that the
instant you have taken a decisive vote in favor of the
Constitution, you send an express to me at Poughkeepsie. Let him take the *shortest route* to that place,
change horses on the road, and use all possible diligence.
I shall with pleasure defray all expenses, and give a
liberal reward to the person. As I suspect an effort will
be made to precipitate us, all possible *safe* dispatch on
your part, as well to obtain a decision as to communicate
the intelligence of it, will be desirable.

United States History, LOSSING

State seal of New Hampshire

Two days later, Hamilton, writing to James Madison in Virginia, speculated on the course of events in the New York campaign for ratification.

[New York, June 8, 1788]

[The Antifederal party] have a majority of two thirds in the Convention and according to the best estimate I can form of about four sevenths in the community. The views of the leaders in this City are pretty well ascertained to be turned towards a *long* adjournment say till next spring or Summer. Their incautious ones observe that this will give an opportunity to the state to *see how the government works and to act according to circumstances.*

My reasonings on the fact are to this effect. The leaders of the party hostile to the constitution are equally hostile to the Union. They are however afraid to reject the constitution at once because that step would bring matters to a crisis between this state and the states which had adopted the Constitution and between the parties in the state. A separation of the Southern district from the other part of the state it is perceived would become the object of the Foederalists and of the two neighbouring states. They therefore resolve upon a long adjournment as the safest and most artful course to effect their final purpose....

For my own part the more I can penetrate the views of the Antifoederal party in this state, the more I dread the consequences of the non adoption of the Constitution by any of the other states, the more I fear an eventual disunion and civil war. God grant that Virginia may accede. Her example will have a vast influence on our politics. New Hampshire, all accounts give us to expect, will be an assenting state.

The Critical Period. FISKE

A view of Poughkeepsie, New York, seen from across the Hudson River

The Federalist advantage at Poughkeepsie would be time. If New Hampshire or Virginia became the ninth state to ratify it, the Constitution would be the law of the land. On June 17, the New York Convention met. George Clinton was named chairman and rules were adopted. To insure delay, Hamilton and Robert R. Livingston drafted a resolution providing that no vote would be taken on the Constitution until all its articles had been considered "Clause by Clause." Two days later, Hamilton sent a terse note to Madison, who faced strong Antifederal opposition in his own convention in Virginia.

[Poughkeepsie, New York, June 19, 1788]
Yesterday, My Dear Sir, The Convention made a house.
That day and this have been spent in preliminary arrangements. Tomorrow we go into a Committee of the
whole on the Constitution. There is every appearance
that a full discussion will take place, which will keep us
together at least a fortnight. It is not easy to conjecture
what will be the result. Our adversaries greatly outnum-
ber us. The leaders gave indications of a pretty desperate
disposition in private conversations previous to the meeting; but I imagine the minor partisans have their scruples
and an air of moderation is now assumed. So far the thing
is not to be despaired of. A happy issue with you must
have considerable influence upon us.

The decision to discuss the Constitution in detail turned
the convention into a debating society in which "Antis" and "Feds" delivered
long orations to prove their points. Nothing could have suited Hamilton and
his friends better: Federalist delegates were skilled public speakers and
might be able to overshadow their opposition, but most important, this pro-
cedure took time. In his first speech, Hamilton answered Antifederalists
who had minimized the national crisis. He opened with a theme that he
used during the whole convention—that the Confederation could not and
should not be revised, and that only the new Constitution would protect
America's liberties and independence.

[Poughkeepsie, New York, June 20, 1788]
What then shall we do? Shall we take the Old Confederation, as the basis of a new system? Can this be
the object of the gentlemen? certainly not. Will any man
who entertains a wish for the safety of his country, trust
the sword and the purse with a single Assembly organized
on principles so defective—so rotten? Though we might
give to such a government certain powers with safety,
yet to give them the full and unlimited powers of taxation
and the national forces would be to establish a despotism;
the definition of which is, a government, in which all
power is concentred in a single body. To take the Old
Confederation, and fashion it upon these principles,
would be establishing a power which would destroy the
liberties of the people. These considerations show clearly,
that a government totally different must be instituted.
They had weight in the convention who formed the new
system. It was seen, that the necessary powers were too

great to be trusted to a single body: They therefore formed two branches; and divided the powers, that each might be a check upon the other. This was the result of their wisdom; and I presume that every reasonable man will agree to it.

The next morning, Hamilton continued his speech and answered the objections of Antifederalists who feared that the House would be too small to represent America's diverse interests. Specifically, critics in the convention proposed that each congressman be elected from a district with twenty thousand inhabitants, not thirty thousand as the Constitution provided.

[Poughkeepsie, New York, June 21, 1788] I would ask, by what rule or reasoning it is determined, that one man is a better representative for twenty than thirty thousand? . . . I agree with the gentleman, that a very small number might give some colour for suspicion: I acknowledge, that ten would be unsafe; on the other hand, a thousand would be too numerous. But I ask him, why will not ninety-one be an adequate and safe representation? This at present appears to be the proper medium. Besides, the President of the United States will be himself the representative of the people. From the competition that ever subsists between the branches of government, the President will be induced to protect their rights, whenever they are invaded by either branch. On whatever side we view this subject, we discover various and powerful checks to the encroachments of Congress. The true and permanent interests of the members are opposed to corruption: Their number is vastly too large for easy combination: The rivalship between the houses will forever prove an insuperable obstacle: The people have an obvious and powerful protection in their own State governments: Should any thing dangerous be attempted, these bodies of perpetual observation, will be capable of forming and conducting plans of regular opposition. Can we suppose the people's love of liberty will not, under the incitement of their legislative leaders, be roused into resistance, and the madness of tyranny be extinguished at a blow? Sir, the danger is too distant, it is beyond all rational calculations. . . .

[Hamilton hammered away at the basic theme of his

Antifederalist Melancton Smith was known as "Mr. Hamilton's most persevering and formidable opponent" in the New York State ratifying convention.

convention speeches—the delegates must examine real problems and discard old prejudices.]

Sir, we hear constantly a great deal, which is rather calculated to awake our passions, and create prejudices, than to conduct us to truth, and teach us our real interests. I do not suppose this to be the design of the gentlemen. Why then are we told so often of an aristocracy? For my part, I hardly know the meaning of this word as it is applied. If all we hear be true, this government is really a very bad one. But who are the aristocracy among us? Where do we find men elevated to a perpetual rank above their fellow citizens; and possessing powers entirely independent of them? The arguments of the gentlemen only go to prove that there are men who are rich, men who are poor, some who are wise, and others who are not—That indeed every distinguished man is an aristocrat.

Revolution, LOSSING

The New York State Convention of 1788 met at the Van Kleek house, then a tavern, at Poughkeepsie.

Hamilton's speech did not convince George Clinton, who still insisted that the Congress was not "comprehensive" enough and that "there will be more safety in the state than in the federal government." Parrying the Governor's thrust, Hamilton accused Clinton of seeking to destroy the Union.

[Poughkeepsie, New York, June 21, 1788] [This] is a species of reasoning, sometimes used to excite popular jealousies, but . . . I do not suppose that the honorable member who advanced the idea, had any such design: He, undoubtedly, would not wish to extend his argument to the destruction of union or government; but this, Sir, is its real tendency. It has been asserted, that the interests, habits and manners of the Thirteen States are different; and hence it is inferred, that no general free government can suit them. . . . I acknowledge, that the local interests of the states are in some degree various; and that there is some difference in their habits and manners: But this I will presume to affirm; that, from New-Hampshire to Georgia, the people of America are as uniform in their interests and manners, as those of any established in Europe. This diversity, to the eye of a speculatist, may afford some marks of characteristic discrimination, but cannot form an impediment to the regular operation of those general powers, which the

Constitution gives to the united government.... Though the difference of interests may create some difficulty and apparent partiality, in the first operations of government, yet the same spirit of accommodation, which produced the plan under discussion, would be exercised in lessening the weight of unequal burthens. Add to this that, under the regular and gentle influence of general laws, these varying interests will be constantly assimilating, till they embrace each other, and assume the same complexion.

When Clinton replied that he was as firm a believer in the Union as any man, Hamilton blandly denied that he had ever said anything to the contrary.

[Poughkeepsie, New York, June 21, 1788]
I only rise to observe that the gentleman has misunderstood me. What I meant to express was this; that if we argued from possibilities only; if we reasoned from chances, or an ungovernable propensity to evil, instead of taking into view the controul, which the nature of things, or the form of the constitution provided, the argument would lead us to withdraw all confidence from our fellow-citizens, and discard the chimerical idea of government.

After the convention adjourned for the day, Hamilton had time to reply to the promising reports that he had been receiving from James Madison in Virginia.

[Poughkeepsie, New York, June 21, 1788]
I thank you for your letter... and am glad to learn that you think the chance is in your favour. I hope no disagreeable change may happen. Yet I own I fear something from your indisposition.

Our debate here began on the clause respecting the proportion of representation &c. which has taken up two days. Tomorrow I imagine we shall talk about the power over elections. The only good information I can give you is that we shall be sometime together and take the chance of events.

The object of the party at present is undoubtedly conditional amendments. What effect events may have cannot precisely be foreseen.

I believe the adoption by New Hampshire is certain.

The movement for "conditional" ratification was unmistakable. As delegates debated each article, conditional amendments were proposed. On June 24, for instance, in an examination of the section pertaining to the Senate, an Antifederalist suggested that no man be allowed to serve two consecutive terms in the upper house and that state legislatures be empowered to "recall" their United States Senators. In rebuttal, Hamilton explained the nature and functions of the Senate.

[Poughkeepsie, New York, June 24, 1788]
In the commencement of a revolution, which received its birth from the usurpations of tyranny, nothing was more natural, than that the public mind should be influenced by an extreme spirit of jealousy.... In forming our confederation, this passion alone seemed to actuate us, and we appear to have had no other view than to secure ourselves from despotism.... But, Sir, there is another object, equally important, and which our enthusiasm rendered us little capable of regarding. I mean a principle of strength and stability in the organization of our government, and vigor in its operations. This purpose could never be accomplished but by the establishment of some select body, formed peculiarly upon this principle. There are few positions more demonstrable than that there should be in every republic, some permanent body to correct the prejudices, check the intemperate passions, and regulate the fluctuations of a popular assembly....

Now, Sir, what is the tendency of the proposed amendment? To take away the stability of government by depriving the senate of its permanency: To make this body subject to the same weakness and prejudices, which are incident to popular assemblies, and which it was instituted to correct; and by thus assimilating the complexion of the two branches, destroy the balance between them. The amendment will render the senator a slave to all the capricious humors among the people.... [Thus] he never can possess that firmness which is necessary to the discharge of his great duty to the union.

According to this 1788 newspaper cartoon, Virginia's approval of the Constitution would bring a New York vote for ratification.

On June 25, the Poughkeepsie Convention learned that New Hampshire had ratified the Constitution—the Confederation was dead. Still, New York Antifederalists balked at unconditional approval. That day, Hamilton wrote to Madison in Virginia.

[New York, June 25, 1788]
I am very sorry to find by your letter...that your

prospects are so critical. Our chance of success here is infinitely slender, and none at all if you go wrong. The leaders of the Antifederalists finding their part seems somewhat squeamish about rejection, are obliged *at present* to recur to the project of conditional amendments. We are going on very deliberately in the discussion and hitherto not without effect.

Even though the Constitution had been ratified by nine states, the convention at Poughkeepsie continued to consider each clause at a stately pace. When the delegates reached the article on taxation, an amendment was introduced limiting Congress to laying imposts and excise taxes on foreign goods. Hamilton's reply to the proposal revealed his growing impatience.

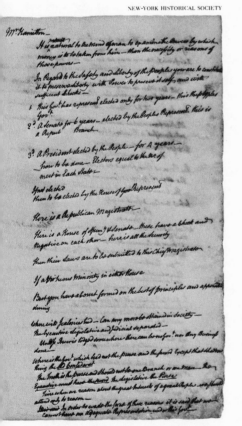

The notes of John McKesson, the convention secretary, on Hamilton's remarks of June 27, 1788.

[Poughkeepsie, New York, June 27, 1788] It is more easy for the human mind to calculate the evils, than the advantages of a measure; and vastly more natural to apprehend the danger, than to see the necessity, of giving powers to our rulers. Hence I may justly expect, that those who hear me, will place less confidence in those arguments which oppose, than in those which favour, their prepossessions.

After all our doubts, our suspicions and speculations ... we must return at last to this important truth—that when we have formed a constitution upon free principles, when we have given a proper balance to the different branches of administration, and fixed representation upon pure and equal principles, we may with safety furnish it with all the powers, necessary to answer, in the most ample manner, the purposes of government.... Now what do gentlemen mean by coming forward and declaiming against this government? Why do they say we ought to limit its powers, to disable it, and to destroy its capacity of blessing the people? Has philosophy suggested—has experience taught, that such a government ought not to be trusted with every thing necessary for the good of society? Sir, when you have divided and nicely balanced the departments of government; When you have strongly connected the virtue of your rulers with their interest; when, in short, you have rendered your system as perfect as human forms can be; you must place confidence; you must give power.

On the same day, Hamilton wrote to Madison. If Virginia's convention, with a strong Antifederalist faction, voted for ratification, opposition in New York might well collapse.

[Poughkeepsie, New York, June 27, 1788]
A day or two ago General Schuyler at my request sent forward to you an express with an account of the adoption of the Constitution by New Hampshire. We eagerly wait for further intelligence from you, as our only chance of success depends on you. There are some slight symptoms of relaxation in some of the leaders; which authorises a gleam of hope, if you do well; but certainly I think not otherwise.

While waiting for word from Madison, Hamilton carried on his fight against the conditional amendment on taxation. One New York newspaper had already described him as standing "under the federal banner...a political porcupine, armed at all points." But in the middle of the debates on taxation, John Lansing, another New York delegate to the Philadelphia Convention, raised an embarrassing point. He charged that the year before, in Philadelphia, Hamilton had demanded that the states be reduced to "mere corporations," whereas he was now telling the Poughkeepsie Convention that these local governments were necessary parts of the new government. The *Daily Advertiser* carried this account of "the altercation."

[Poughkeepsie, New York, June 28, 1788]
This called up Mr. Hamilton, who entered into a statement of facts; denied what the gentleman had asserted; declared that in the General Convention his ideas had been uniformly the same as on the present occasion: that tho' he at that time declared, as he had constantly and publicly done since, his apprehension that the State governments would finally subvert the general system, unless the arm of the Union was more strengthened than it was even by this Constitution; yet he had through the whole of the business advocated the preservation of the State governments, and affirmed them to be useful and necessary. He accused Mr. Lansing's insinuation as improper, unbecoming and uncandid. Mr. Lansing rose, and with much spirit resented the imputation. He made an appeal to Judge [Robert] Yates, who had taken notes in the Federal Convention for a proof of Mr. Hamilton's expressions. This produced some disorder ...and the Chairman was obliged to call to order.

On June 30, Robert Yates read the notes of Hamilton's speeches in Philadelphia, quoting Hamilton's use of the term "corporate powers" for the states. The *Daily Advertiser* reported the way in which Hamilton and John Jay soothed the Antifederalists.

[Poughkeepsie, New York, June 30, 1788]
Mr. Hamilton observed, that corporate was an ambiguous term, and asked Mr. Yates if he understood that he (Mr. Hamilton) used it as descriptive of powers, similar to those of the city of New-York? To which Mr. Yates answered in the negative; adding that he understood the gentleman not to wish such a privation of powers as would reduce the States to mere corporations in the popular acceptation of that term; but only such as would prevent the Members from retarding in any degree, the operations of the united government. Col. Hamilton then asked him if he did not, after the above mentioned debate in the Federal Convention, hear him (Col. Hamilton) say, that his opinion was that the State governments ought to be supported, and that they would be useful and necessary: and further asked him if he did not remember that he (Col. Hamilton) had recommended (as an additional security to the States governments) a Court of Impeachments, to be composed by the Chief Judges of the several States, together with the Chief Justice of the United States. To all which Mr. Yates gave an affirmative answer. On Mr. Jay's proposing to Mr. Yates some questions with a view to set the matter in the most explicit point of light, Mr. Yates answered as before, that Col. Hamilton's design did not appear to him to point at a total extinguishment of the State governments, but only to deprive them of the means of impeding the operation of the Union.

John Lansing, Jr., compiled and published Robert Yates's notes of the secret debates taken at the Philadelphia Convention.

By the beginning of July, Hamilton still had no news from Virginia on that convention's decision. Again, he wrote to Madison.

[Poughkeepsie, New York, July 2, 1788]
Your letter of the 20th. came to hand two days since. I regret that your prospects were not yet reduced to greater certainty. There is more and more reason to believe that our conduct will be influenced by yours.

Our discussions have not yet travelled beyond the power of taxation. To day we shall probably quit this ground to pass to another. Our arguments confound, but do not convince. Some of the leaders however appear to me to be convinced *by circumstances* and to be desirous of a retreat. This does not apply to the Chief, who wishes to establish *Clintonism* on the basis of *Antifoederalism.*

As Hamilton had predicted, "circumstances," not "arguments," turned the tide at Poughkeepsie. At noon on July 2, a messenger from New York City interrupted Governor Clinton's speech to announce that Virginia had ratified the Constitution. A few days later, Hamilton reported to Madison that there were signs that the solid Antifederalist front had weakened.

[New York, July 8, 1788]

I felicitate you sincerely on the event in Virginia; but my satisfaction will be allayed, if I discover too much facility in the business of amendment-making. I fear the system will be wounded in some of its vital parts by too general a concurrence in some very injudicious recommendations. . . .

We yesterday *passed* through the constitution. To day some definitive proposition is to be brought forward; but what we are at a loss to judge. We have good reason to believe that our opponents are not agreed, and this affords some ground of hope. Different things are thought of—*Conditions precedent*, or previous amendments; Conditions *subsequent*, or the proposition of amendments upon condition, that if they are not adopted within a limited time, the state shall be at liberty to *withdraw* from the Union, and lastly *recommendatory amendments*. In either case *constructive declarations* will be carried as far as possible. We will go as far as we can in the latter without invalidating the act, and will concur in rational recommendations. The rest for our opponents.

A broadside printed at Poughkeepsie announced Virginia's ratification of the Constitution, June 25, 1788

The next day, the Antifederalists introduced a list of fifty-five amendments to the Constitution arranged under three headings: explanatory, conditional, and recommendatory. Jay introduced a resolution, drafted by Hamilton, that eliminated the "conditional" category, but Antifederalists resisted this move. Hamilton and Jay argued that a ratification with "conditions" would have no force. The *Daily Advertiser* carried this sympathetic account of Hamilton's speech.

John Jay: a 1781 engraving, after a portrait "drawn from the life"

[Poughkeepsie, New York, July 12, 1788]

He described in a delicate but most affecting manner the various ungenerous attempts to prejudice the minds of the Convention against him. He had been represented as "an ambitious man, a man unattached to the interests and insensible to the feelings of the people"; and even his supposed talents had been wrested to his dishonor, and produced as a charge against his integrity and virtue. He called on the world to point out an instance in which he had ever deviated from the line of public or private duty. The pathetic appeal fixed the silent sympathetic gaze of the spectators, and made them all his own.

He then proceeded to refute the fallacious reasonings of opposition.... He proved, in the first place, from the series of papers on which the authority of the present Convention was founded, that it had no possible decisive power, but to adopt or reject absolutely: that it had indeed a power to recommend ... but it had none to dictate to or embarrass the union by any restrictions or conditions whatever: that the Committee was not a body commissioned to tender stipulations or form a compact, but to dissent from or agree to a plan of government, which could be altered either in its form or exercise only by an authority equal in all respects, to the one which gave it existence. Having made this point clear, he went on to shew that the future Congress would have no authority to receive us into the union on such terms: that this conditional adoption included evidently a disagreement to and rejection of a part of the Constitution: that Congress ... must consider such a partial rejection in the light of a total one....

Mr. Hamilton ... entreated the Convention in a pathetic strain to make a solemn pause, and weigh well what they were about to do, before they decided on a subject so infinitely important. The orator then closed his address, and received from every unprejudiced spectator the murmur of admiration and applause.

A week later, trying another tactic, Hamilton and his allies introduced a resolution for adjournment to permit delegates to learn "the Sentiments at present entertained by their Constituents." As both sides knew, these "Sentiments" were now in favor of ratification. On July 17,

Gilbert Livingston, an Antifederalist, made frantic notes of Hamilton's speech before the convention.

[Poughkeepsie, New York, July 17, 1788]

Hamilton: [There are] scarce any new reasons to be offered—they are short & must have their force. It may do good—[it] cannot do evil. While men *hope*, they never become enraged. Both parties hope to succeed, therefore [they] will not heat. Things have changed since we came here. Therefore [it is] decent we should consult our constituents. Good may come, & no evil can come. . . .

[There is a] difference of Opinion respecting the supposed defect. [Some] Gentlemen look at it only to find out the defects and not to discover its securities—& beauties. [It] turns on this, that [the] gentlemen say the state governments will be destroyed. He says they are necessary, & that they will be preserved.

[Hamilton] supposes that if the adoption takes place as proposed we are out of the Union. Some may think we may then enjoy our impost &c., but [Hamilton] lays it down the Union will not permit us to remain so because their interest & safety will not permit it.

H amilton's speech was interrupted. When he resumed, he made a forceful point by reading a letter from James Madison, written on June 30. Madison reported that Virginia's Antifederalists had decided against appealing to the people over the state convention's decision to ratify the Constitution. If Virginians were content to trust the new government to provide the Constitution with necessary amendments, New York "Antis" had lost vital support. Gilbert Livingston jotted down Hamilton's comments —a series of embarrassing questions for Clinton's supporters.

[Poughkeepsie, New York, July 17, 1788]

Now, what have we to hope for from other states? Assistance? Against what—will they assist us to oppose themselves?

Can we compare our strength against the whole? They will have the power of government and the wealth of the whole country against us; the sea ports [are] all for them. Is there hope of prevailing in so unequal a contest?

Whence are we to derive means of assistance? [From] foreign powers? Whom—France or great Brittain? France is the Ally of the United States. Great Brittain? What object could she have? [She] has totally given up her claim to this country. Will she take the weaker by the hand, to oppose the stronger? Who would wish again to come under her dominion? But she never will because [she has] no interest by it.

This [is] not all. We are divided among our selves: the southern district [is] warmly attached to this government. This [is] a fact and a sentiment which will increase.... Is it in the power of the Northern [district] to compel the southern? [This is] impracticable—they will be aided & protected by the Union. [Hamilton] hopes the election of separation will never be made, [but] it will take place if we reject the Constitution....

... Will Congress overcome the obstacles to receive us? They will not. They are jealous of us and view us as a selfish sister—our neighbours nearest especially.... Their interest in having us with them will be diminished by considering that they can have our [southern] part—the chief source of wealth....

Pause—and suppose the minorities in the other states would go with us to resist. Is this desirable—to have the country divided into martial bands? Who will command? In this case, at any rate, adieu to liberty; a despotism will follow. Can any man wish to run this risk? The cause of republicanism should induce us to avoid this....

[There are] distinguished patriots on both sides, though most [are] for the government: [John] Hancock acquiesces though in a situation that might tempt him to oppose it; [John] Adams—he first conceived the bold idea of independence—he is for it; Governor [William] Livingston, born a republican, he [is] for it; Franklin, this old grey headed patriot looking into the grave, approves it; General Washington came forward. Disinterested, [he] hazarded all without reward. All parties, Whigs and Tories, admired and put confidence in him. At the close of the war, at the head of a discontented army, did he take advantage of the situation of the army or country? No, he proved himself a patriot. This man came forward again and hazarded his harvest of glory. In this case he saw the work he had been engaged in was but half finished. He came forward and approved this Constitution. Is it in human nature to suppose that these good men should lose their virtue and acquiesce in a government that is substantially defective to the liberties of their country?...

Our sister states invite us. They have been as jealous

Portrait of James Madison, based on a painting by Charles Willson Peale

of their liberty as we....All mankind [invites us]. Heaven patronized us—it now invites us.

Is it not wonderful that ten states should adopt it? Let us take care not to oppose the whole country. If [we were] on the verge of eternity, [Hamilton] would exhort us to union.

Antifederalists brought forward another plan—an unconditional ratification under which New York retained the right to secede from the Union if her conditions were not met. Hamilton wrote to James Madison, who had recently joined the Congress in New York City, for his opinion of the new plan.

The "Federal Ship," named in honor of Hamilton, is paraded through the streets of New York to celebrate ratification of the Constitution.

[Poughkeepsie, New York, July 19, 1788] Let me know your idea of the possibility of our being *received* on that plan. You will understand that the only qualification will be *the reservation* of a right to recede in case our amendments have not been decided upon in one of the modes pointed out in the Constitution within a certain number of years, perhaps five or seven.

If this can in the first instance be admitted as a ratification I do not fear any further consequences. Congress will I presume recommend certain amendments to render the *structure* of the government more secure. This will satisfy the more considerate and honest opposers of the constitution, and with the aid of time will break up the party.

While Hamilton awaited Madison's reply, he described deliberations at Poughkeepsie as "debating on amendments without having decided what is to be done with them." At last, on July 23, Melancton Smith and Samuel Jones broke with other "Antis" to introduce motions for ratification "in full Confidence" that the conditional amendments would be added. Their proposals passed by two votes. John Lansing insisted this ratification still included the right of secession if the amendments were not adopted. Hamilton had just received Madison's opinion that this "reservation" would invalidate the ratification. Gilbert Livingston made notes of Hamilton's speech.

[Poughkeepsie, New York, July 24, 1788] Hamilton was in hopes this Morning of Unanimity when this Motion was first mentioned...[but] since thinks otherwise. [He] has taken advice with men of character: they think it will not do. [He] proposed to read a Letter

Hamilton (second column) was among those who signed the New York Convention's act of ratification.

[from James Madison]. [He] reads it. [He] supposes this adoption [is] conditional.... The terms of the constitution import a perpetual compact between the different states; this certainly is not. Treaties and engagements with foreign nations are perpetual; this cannot be under this adoption.... States & men are averse to inequality. They [are] fully bound & we partially.

Should we risk so much on so little? Motives of expediency [are] too much relied on.... Is it not of importance that we join unanimously to procure a convention? The observation of Lansing does not meet the objection as they [the other states] will contemplate wheather this is a ratification. If they have any doubt, they will appoint Congress to meet on certain federal ground. [The] interest of some states [is] against us. If they are driven away by us the people will be dissatisfied &ct.

We have done everything which possibly can insure our wish. This we shall loose by a second state convention. We shall not be represented in Congress & this for no real end. [Hamilton] moves to have the question postponed & that a circular letter be wrote.

Madison's opinion could not be ignored. Hamilton's "circular letter" helped the Antifederalists save face, and on July 25, Lansing's motion on the right of secession was defeated, 31 to 28. By the same margin, the convention agreed to ratify, "in full Confidence" that their list of essential amendments would be enacted. Unanimously they accepted a draft of a circular letter to be sent to the other states concerning the defects of the Constitution. This letter, written by John Jay, with some corrections by Hamilton, was dispatched the next day.

Poughkeepsie, New York, July 26, 1788. "We the members of the Convention of this State, have deliberately & maturely considered the Constitution proposed for the united States. Several articles in it appear so exceptionable to a majority of us, that nothing but the fullest confidence of obtaining a Revision of them by a general convention, and an invincible Reluctance to separating from our Sister States could have prevailed upon a sufficient number to ratify it without stipulating for previous amendments. We all unite in opinion that such a Revision will be necessary to recommend it to the approbation and Support of a numorous Body of our constituents."

It is impossible to point to one isolated incident to prove that Hamilton won the fight for ratification in New York, but it would be equally difficult to imagine how the battle could have been won without him. Colonel Hamilton, that "political porcupine," was always at work. Although *The Federalist* convinced few New Yorkers, its continued publication kept the issues before the public. And although Hamilton's party lost the election in New York, his correspondence with leaders in other states enabled Federalists at Poughkeepsie to plan a strategy by which they prevailed over an Antifederalist majority. A bit arrogant, much too sure of himself, Hamilton could not be ignored. When the time came, he showed enough political sense to withdraw and let his friend Jay conciliate the convention and carry the day for ratification.

Hamilton's role in championing the Constitution was widely recognized in his own day. Three days before the Poughkeepsie Convention adjourned, the city of New York held a belated celebration of the ratification of the Constitution by nine states with a "Grand Fœderal Procession," costing almost ten thousand pounds. The date of the parade had been postponed from July 4 until July 23 so that a "Federal Ship" could be constructed. The ship was pulled along Broadway "with floating sheets, and full sails," and her name was *Hamilton*, to honor the man who had signed the Constitution at Philadelphia for New York and who was still fighting the good fight at Poughkeepsie. In the drizzling rain that Wednesday in July, the painted colors of the *Hamilton*'s flag smeared and ran, but the "Federal Ship" still helped give the parade "a very pompous appearance." Similarly, one Federalist remarked that the Constitution had "undergone an ordeal [by] torture" at Poughkeepsie, but was "preserved, as by fire." Federalism had survived. New York had become the "eleventh pillar" of the new government.

It seemed that there was nothing left for Hamilton to do but insure that the "factions" that had arisen during the Confederacy and rallied under the banner of Antifederalism would be destroyed. The Federalist ship needed a loyal crew and proper officers. For Hamilton, this meant that George Washington must lead the nation and that George Clinton must be replaced as Governor of New York.